The Forgiveness Handbook

A Simple Guide to Freedom of the Mind and Heart

CLIFFORD B. EDWARDS

Empower People Ventures
PO Box 179098
San Diego, CA 92177

ISBN: 978-0-9895452-1-1
Library of Congress Control Number: 2013942661
Produced in the United States of America

The Forgiveness Handbook

A Simple Guide to Freedom of the Mind and Heart

Dedication

This book is dedicated to the late Debbie Ford: a brilliant author, trainer and friend who left this world far too early. It is due to her teaching, mentoring and support that this book is able to exist.

Preface

Hello and Welcome Reader,

I wrote and assembled this book for you. Yes, you - the one reading these words right now. I knew you'd be here. I knew that you might want and need the concepts, ideas and answers discussed in this book. Well, okay, not necessarily you personally. But you as part of the collective - one of the billions of people alive on the planet right now who can benefit from understanding and practicing forgiveness more fully. One who still carries a burden of emotions and beliefs from events in your past. Someone desiring more than what you currently seem able to allow into your life.

As a human being, you have previously experienced hurtful incidents and situations in your life. You will likely continue to have painful, regrettable or unwanted experiences as you move forward. As a result, you've already made some kinds of negative, limiting, long-lasting beliefs about yourself and others and you'll be prone to making more in the future. That means unless you're a forgiveness ninja and you have faithfully remained aware of and absolved yourself and others of every transgression - large or small - each and every day of your life, then you have something that needs to be forgiven.

Don't believe me? Okay, if you can relate to or admit to any of the following circumstances or situations, then this book is for you.

1   If you at least sometimes make negative judgments about yourself and others.

2   If you're holding onto any degree of regret, remorse, sorrow, guilt or shame about your actions, decisions or circumstances past or present.

3   If you still carry – however well hidden – any anger, resentment, blame or righteous indignation toward some other person or group.

4   If there are people in your life whom you hate, strongly dislike or feel any kind of animosity toward.

5   If the thought of being with a specific person or group of people makes you feel uncomfortable, irritated, queasy or upset.

6   If you feel superior to or better than some other person or group of people.

7   If you find yourself needing to be right and defend your opinions at all costs or being argumentative, dismissive or resistant with others.

8   If you lack self-confidence, feel inherently shameful, bad or that there's something wrong with you.

9   If you habitually put the wants, needs and desires of others ahead of your own well-being.

10   If you often feel suspicious of people's motives or can't trust others at all.

11   If you experience an ongoing negative, judgmental, shaming or blaming internal dialog.

12 If you have fantasies of revenge or retribution toward any person or organization that hurt you in the past.

13 If you find yourself habitually not following through with plans and commitments, being self-destructive or self-sabotaging in any way.

14 If you have any areas in your life that aren't working as you want, no matter what you try to do to improve them.

Can you relate to or admit to any of the conditions above? Everything on that list is an indication that you have something in your past or present that needs to be forgiven. You can think of them as symptoms of undigested and unresolved emotions, judgments or beliefs from your past. This is just a partial list too. There are many more symptoms we might add to the list – those I included are just some of the more common and overt of them.

As a life coach and transformational trainer over the past dozen years, I've been involved in many conversations about and explorations of forgiveness. In that time, I've learned a lot about non-forgiveness as well. I've come to realize how subtle yet pervasive some of the signs of non-forgiveness are. Any little judgment, any little emotional twinge, pang or flutter, any little arrogant, righteous or defensive thought, word or action can serve as an entry point for discovering a hidden hurt, a buried resentment or some long-forgotten shame or guilt that can be brought to the surface, compassionately examined and forgiven.

It's useful to consider how you feel about yourself when you're experiencing any of the symptoms in the list above.

1. Do you feel good about yourself?

2. Do you feel productive, creative and contributive?

3. Do you feel open, joyful and connected?

4. Are you energized, vital and alive?

5. Are you motivated to unabashedly go after your dreams and desires?

Based on my own experience, the answer I'd venture on your behalf is "probably not." When you're in the grip of any unresolved, undigested incident from the past, it's unlikely that you're able to be the kind of person that you really want to be.

I've written this book to help stimulate both conversation about and the practice of forgiveness. One of my intentions is to help point out the high cost of neglecting or declining to forgive. There are the costs of unhappiness, dissatisfaction and a nagging sense of regret. But there are many others affecting all realms of your life – mental, emotional, physical, financial and spiritual. Non-forgiveness comes with a cost of broken relationships, shattered self-esteem, wasted time and energy, divided families, crushed dreams, depression, stress, worry, fear and so much more. If you're committed to having more success, happiness and fulfillment in your life, then holding onto the grievances of the past is a cost that you can't afford to bear any longer.

If I've successfully convinced you of the high cost of non-forgiveness, then I'd also like you to recognize that the rewards of forgiving are as lofty as the cost of non-forgiveness is destructive. There are the benefits of peace of mind, clarity of purpose, an open heart, love and connection, a renewed sense of motivation and desire, enhanced levels of energy, creativity, joy, and so much more. But perhaps most importantly, and this is something that I'll emphasize throughout the book in many ways, forgiveness equates to freedom. Forgiveness grants you freedom from the cruel patterns of judgmental, blaming thoughts. It liberates you from the oppressive burdens of unresolved emotions and the chafing restrictions of limiting beliefs from the past. Forgiveness gives you the freedom to more fully be and become a unique, whole and unbridled expression of yourself.

So this book is for you if you have suffered hurtful, painful, wounding or upsetting events and experiences of any sort in your life. It is for you if you have any questions about what forgiveness is and why you should expend the mental, emotional or spiritual energy to forgive anything or anyone. This book is designed to be a handbook, a place where you can come for ideas, reminders and perspectives on forgiveness. It's designed to emphasize the fundamental concepts and ideas about forgiving and to stress the benefits of doing so. Its intent is to inspire, motivate, encourage and cajole you into adopting and keeping a regular practice of forgiveness in your life.

This book is structured as a series of answers to some of the commonly asked questions or commonly held assumptions about forgiveness. As you'll hear me stress many times and in many ways throughout the various chapters, forgiveness is a crucial part of living a life that's productive, fulfilling, enjoyable and open to new possibilities. Choosing to forgive is also choosing to love yourself and others more fully.

To help and encourage you along the way, I have some bonuses and added value for you. I've sprinkled in a few links to worksheets, quotes, blog posts, special videos and other items that will help you in your personal process of forgiveness. Some of this free additional material is publicly available; some is reserved just for readers of *The Forgiveness Handbook*. So read on, and give the perspectives, suggestions and exercises a try. The only things you've got to lose are the pains and limitations of your past.

Cliff

If you want to read and learn more about me or about forgiveness, go to: www.forgivenessclub.com.

Table of Contents

Chapter 7

Chapter 8

Chapter 9

Chapter 10

Chapter 11

Introduction

Thank You

I want to start by thanking you for investing your money, time and energy in this book. In addition, thank you in advance for taking the time to read, digest and put into practice the ideas and concepts in this book.

But my real hope and desire is that the person ultimately thanking you for taking the time to read, digest and put into practice the ideas and concepts in this book is you. And maybe your partner or spouse, or your family, or your friends, colleagues and co-workers will thank you too. That's because what's available to you through choosing to practice forgiveness of self and others is truly amazing. It really is. And that brings us to the promise that this book – and the information in it – holds for you.

A Bold Promise

In *The Forgiveness Handbook*, I'll share with you the secret to freedom of the mind and heart. I'm going to tell you how you can live a much happier, more fulfilling and self-expressed life. You'll gain insights and perspectives that can allow you to release your daily burden of stress, anxiety and fear. This book can challenge you to lighten your load emotionally, mentally and spiritually. It can nudge you to reclaim your sense of curiosity, adventure and enthusiasm for life. You'll discover an effective means of escaping the tyranny of an incessantly repetitive, negative, judgmental and demeaning internal dialog. It can offer a reliable means for leaving behind any last shreds of a victim mentality or lingering belief that you're not worthy of having what you desire.

Through digesting and integrating the ideas in this book, you can come to understand how to have more harmonious and respectful interactions with those around you. You can foster more loving, authentic and connected relationships with family and friends. The concepts herein can enable you to live more fully present in the moment, free of nagging thoughts of guilt, shame, regret and doubt that drag your awareness into the darkness of past mistakes and misfortune. At the same time, it can instruct you how to equip yourself with greater levels of wisdom, compassion and understanding while preparing you to create and have more of what you most want in the future.

Am I overstating what you can get out of reading this book? Not at all. Everything I've described - and more - is available through understanding and committing to the practice of forgiveness. You may have noticed that I used the word "can" a lot in describing what's available. That's because it's up to *you* how you choose to read and interact with the contents of the book. In order to fulfill that bold promise, to get all that I've mentioned and more, you can't just read the book. You also have to be willing to open your mind and heart to new ways of thinking and different ways of viewing things. You have to be willing to act on the ideas you encounter and compel yourself to take on forgiveness as you never have before.

When I talk about forgiveness in this context, I'm talking about real forgiveness - deep and complete forgiveness of yourself and others. It's forgiveness that comes from the caring, authenticity of your heart rather than the familiar, repetitive machinations of your head. It's a kind of forgiveness that challenges you to go outside of your comfort zone, beyond the boundaries of what you currently know or believe about the painful or hurtful incidents of your past and present. It means being willing to forgive even when you don't want to forgive, even when you think that others don't deserve it. This kind of forgiveness needs to be a daily part of your life. It's something that may take time to develop and mature as a perspective and practice. Are you ready to do that?

I've been a student of forgiveness for many years. Yet over the past year and a half or so, my life has presented circumstances that have prompted me to delve more deeply into the exploration and practice of forgiveness. To do so, I had to choose to open up to new levels of humility, acceptance and understanding. I was required to honestly examine - and at times discard - some of my long-held beliefs about myself and others. I've learned to forgive as I never had before: from a place of heart and feeling, rather than just within my head and mind. All of this has given me a newfound respect for the power and importance of the seemingly simple, yet often forgotten social and emotional construct we call forgiveness.

I've learned that the process of forgiving myself and others is often complex, nuanced and challenging. I've also experienced that the results are always worthwhile, even (maybe especially) when the process took me in directions that I never expected to go. It's been at various times demanding, fulfilling, joyful, painful and always self-revealing. I've developed greater compassion, flexibility of thought and willingness to be more authentic with others. I've also developed new ideas about what forgiveness is and is not, as well as why and how I should choose to forgive. As a result, I now take the bold, hopeful and perhaps naive position that anything - any hurt, any betrayal any offense - can and should be forgiven.

Introduction

I now love talking and sharing about the many different ways of thinking about and understanding forgiveness. This book had its beginnings several months ago in a series of five-minute videos I made titled "Forgiveness FAQ's, The What, Why and How of Forgiveness." Each of the videos addresses a common question about forgiving and forgiveness. (If you're interested, you can still find the original videos here: www.forgivenessclub.com/forgiveness-faqs/.) I transcribed the content of the videos and then fleshed them out with additional stories, explanations and exercises. Some key concepts and ideas are repeated throughout so that each chapter can be read and stand on its own. But you'll get a much more full understanding and satisfying experience if you read them all consecutively.

In the book, I share many of my own experiences along with ideas and perspectives that have been valuable to me in learning to forgive. In the various chapters, I present several different ways and ideas for how to forgive. My intent is that you try them out and see which of the methods or perspectives work for you. Ultimately, my desire is to inspire you to open your heart and mind to the awareness and practice of forgiveness. If you do, then step by step and a day at a time, you will realize the bold promise and experience for yourself the miracles that are available through forgiveness.

How to Get the Most Out of this Book

Chapters and Content

As I mentioned in the Introduction, this book originated as a collection of answers to individual questions about forgiveness, though each are presented in greater depth here than in the original form. As you read through the book you may feel like there is some repetition of the concepts presented. There is, and it is written in this way for very specific reasons:

- Through repetition comes retention. Some of the chapters offer similar concepts and ideas about *what forgiveness is* and *why you should forgive*, yet present them in different contexts and examples. Reading similar information through different lenses will allow you to grasp it more fully and understand it in a more nuanced way.

- In each chapter you'll find somewhat different methods or perspectives for *how to forgive*. You can try out the various methods and see which of them work well for you. Then ideally, you'll be able to more naturally and easily put practices of forgiveness to use in your life day to day.

- Finally and most importantly, this book is meant to be exactly as the title claims: *The Forgiveness Handbook*. It is designed to serve as a reference and an overview of the *what, why* and *how* of forgiveness. With each chapter addressing a specific common question about forgiveness and forgiving, you can pick it up any time and get a quick set of insights and reminders to help you through any challenges you might happen to face from hurtful events of your life past or present.

In this way you can continue to find value in the information and experience all of the benefits available to you through forgiving.

Journaling and Writing Exercises

At the end of every chapter of this book you'll find optional journaling exercises to complete. The exercises are designed to be done in sequence and to build on one another. If you do each of the exercises as you move through the book, you'll end up having completed your own personal process of forgiveness around one or more people or incidents from your life. To get the most out of these writing exercises please keep the following suggestions and guidelines in mind.

- Get a notebook, journal or pad of paper that you can designate as your Forgiveness Journal and use to complete these exercises. Better yet, get *The Forgiveness Handbook Companion Workbook*, a companion for *The Forgiveness Handbook* that I've produced as an additional support for you in the forgiveness process. In *The Forgiveness Handbook Companion Workbook*, you'll find additional questions and step by step prompts to help you get the most value out of the exercises and contemplations. To purchase this companion workbook as either a PDF file or in physical form, go to: www.theforgivenesshandbook.com/workbook.

- Be aware that these exercises are designed to be just for you. They provide you with an opportunity to be completely honest with yourself. So though you may be writing about very personal or sensitive thoughts, feelings or experiences, please give yourself permission to write or share anything that you need to in your personal journal.

- For each exercise, make sure to set aside a block of time to sit down by yourself and in a place where you can be still and quiet with your thoughts. I recommend that you generally set aside at least fifteen to twenty minutes. However, some exercises may require a little less time to complete, while others may require a little longer.

- Prepared with your Companion Workbook (notebook, pad or journal), spend some time with each of the questions in an exercise to reflect, contemplate and allow thoughts and ideas to come to you before you begin to write your answer. Then once you've started writing, give yourself permission to continue free writing beyond the initial answer, to see what else might be revealed through the journaling process.

- The purpose of the journaling exercises is to access wisdom, information and ideas from within your unconscious mind – what some of you might call your inner voice or inner wisdom. Ideally you want to allow the answers to come from beyond the habitual patterns of your conscious mind and usual ways of thinking. So if you find yourself trying or thinking really hard during any exercise, it's an indication that you're in your conscious mind attempting to figure out an answer, rather than simply tuning into the deeper levels of information that are already there.

- The answers that originate in your unconscious mind or inner voice are typically those that flash into your awareness first – almost immediately after reading or asking yourself a question. However, you likely have trained yourself to not pay attention to, ignore, edit or delete those flashes of insight in favor of the more familiar and comfortable beliefs and habitual thought patterns of your conscious mind.

- Any time you become aware there's effort in your thinking and you're trying to come up with an answer, you've probably already ignored or edited out something that came to you from your unconscious. In those situations just stop, relax again, then focus your attention on your breath while allowing yourself to notice the very first impulses of thoughts, images, words or feelings that quickly come to you.

- Don't edit yourself or your ideas during this process; simply write down whatever comes to you even if it doesn't initially seem to make sense. What makes sense to your conscious mind is generally based in what you already know and your habitual thought patterns of the past.

- If a thought, image, word or feeling that quickly comes to you in response to any of the questions doesn't initially make sense, trust that it's likely to have come from your deeper level of awareness. As you move ahead with the exercise or through the exercises, the seemingly strange or nonsensical pieces will fall into place and a more coherent picture will emerge for you.

But no matter how you do the exercises, I strongly encourage you to just make the choice to do them. You'll come away with a deeper understanding of yourself, your past and your ability to forgive. And more importantly you'll lighten your own emotional load and gain greater freedom of your mind and heart.

Chapter 1

What is Forgiveness?

Forgiveness is the fragrance that the violet sheds on the heel that has crushed it.
-Mark Twain

This book is a conversation about forgiveness. Every word and every sentence is here to help point you in the direction of becoming more forgiving, and in the process, gaining more freedom. Forgiveness is one of those things that I often hear people talk about. However, I've noticed that there seems to be more talk about forgiveness than actual forgiving. Through this conversation about forgiveness, you can not only understand what forgiveness is, but most importantly, you can begin to put it more fully into practice in your life and reap the benefits.

We'll start this conversation with the simple question: "What is forgiveness?" As a word geek, I love going to the dictionary to look up words and get definitions of things. I usually have a sense of what most words mean and understand the concepts from my own experience and perspective. But I like to check things out with the dictionaries and get clear, accurate input from the professionals. So I went to the *Merriam Webster Online Dictionary* to look up the word "forgive."

What is Forgiveness?

Forgive

1: a: to give up resentment of or claim to requital for <*forgive* an insult>

b : to grant relief from payment of <*forgive* a debt>

2: to cease to feel resentment against (an offender) : <u>PARDON</u> <*forgive* one's enemies>

Among the definitions, 1:a and 2 stood out particularly and both involve the release of resentment. This is one of the crucial characteristics of forgiveness. Forgiveness means letting go of resentment, blame and judgment. It means letting go of guilt and shame. It's forgiving yourself and forgiving others for anything that you might still feel bad about or have some negative emotional charge around. When you forgive, you let go of a burden, let go of the baggage of the past so that you don't have to drag it around with you any longer.

Take a moment and play a little game of imagination with me.

1   Think about something that you still feel angry about, or maybe that you feel resentful about. Maybe it's about a person or a situation. Maybe it's something that happened years ago. Maybe it's something that took place more recently. Whatever it is, right now bring to mind something that still troubles you – something that you're holding negative judgments about.

2   As you start to think about this troubling event or person, notice what happens in your body. Notice how you feel.

3   Does your body feel comfortable?   Do you feel light, creative, joyful and ready to have fun?

4   Or does your body - like mine when I do this - tighten up, start to feel tense, frustrated or experience churning or knots in your stomach?

5   If you feel any tenseness, tightness or discomfort of any kind, that's an effect of stored anger, resentment, blame, guilt, shame or other negative emotions.

Forgiveness is the act of letting go of those old feelings so that they no longer affect or limit you in any way.

Notice that all it takes to change the way you feel is to change what you're thinking.   When you remember or think about something troubling, it stimulates troubling emotions. Emotions are the physiological response to what occurs in your mind.   The emotions you feel come as a direct result of the thoughts you think and the beliefs you hold.   How you think and what you believe about a person or experience has a simple cause and effect relationship with how you feel about the same.

Meanings and Interpretations

What is forgiveness?   In its largest and perhaps simplest sense, forgiveness means to let go of any negative judgments, and limiting, disempowering, or fearful interpretations and meanings from events of the past or present.   It is an act of claiming your freedom from a self-constructed prison of negative thoughts and beliefs about yourself, others or the world.   From the time you were able to think about and interpret the events of your life, you began to create meanings and beliefs. Some of the experiences felt good and so the meanings and beliefs you made were likely positive and empowering for you. Other incidents felt bad, painful or hurtful in some way, and so the meanings and beliefs you made were likely negative, limiting or disempowering. If you're like 99% of the rest of the people in the world, every time you experienced some sort of painful, traumatic, or highly-charged event, you made a negative interpretation of it. You judged it as wrong or bad and gave it a meaning that left you diminished, shut down, closed off or limited in some way. In doing so you learned to judge your experiences as right or wrong, good or bad. Now it's your own negative judgments that hold in place the emotional charge, bad feelings, resentments, regrets, limiting interpretations and disempowering beliefs from your past. When you shift and release your negative judgments, then everything else is able to easily and naturally drop away as well. Judgments – arising from negative interpretations – are like epoxy resins that form the durable bonds of non-forgiveness.

Here's an example of a negative meaning arising from a past event in my own life. I was about five years old and in the first months of kindergarten. One day, the teacher decided to introduce us to the library, so off we went as a class to this big, strange room. The teacher used the time to take a break and left us alone with the librarian. Like many of the other kids, I felt kind of uncomfortable and fearful there in that unfamiliar place. Pretty soon, I had to go to the bathroom and I didn't know where the bathroom was. I didn't know if I was even allowed to go here. So I waited and I waited and it only got worse. Finally, instead of being brave and raising my hand to ask for help, I just sat there in my little chair and wet myself. My bladder was relieved but at the same time I somehow knew it was the wrong thing to do. So for the rest of the time in the library, I felt embarrassed and shameful.

On the way back to the classroom, I got teased by the other kids. They made fun of me for the wet spot running from my butt all the way down my legs. They teased me about the puddle I'd left under my chair. They chided me and called me names. I just wanted to hide. I felt humiliated, ashamed and like there was no escape. It was just awful.

As a result of that experience, I made an interpretation about myself. I judged it to mean that I had done something bad. The fact that I'd wet my pants in a public place made me feel like there was something wrong with me. I attached a negative judgment and disempowering meaning to the event. I internalized that negative meaning and the sense that I was somehow flawed and turned it into a limiting belief. And I carried that belief around with me well into my adult years.

Time Passes, Beliefs Abide

Although I was no longer conscious of the belief and barely remembered the incident, the meaning I had attached to it and the shame of it became a permanent part of who I was. Along with the remnant embarrassment and humiliation of other similar and later experiences, it worked to dim my light, stifle my innate curiosity and dampen my enthusiasm for life. It caused me to see myself as inferior to others and believe that I had to hide the truth of who I was. So in order to compensate for being bad and flawed, I became a good guy and a people-pleaser. As an adolescent and young adult, I put the needs, wants and desires of others before my own. I hid my perceived unworthiness behind a façade of likeability, competence and cool detachment.

The meanings that I gave to that experience and the beliefs that went along with it profoundly influenced the course and quality of my life for many years. [The belief that there was something wrong with me, coupled with the shame and humiliation of that experience, constantly gnawed at my self-esteem and left me feeling undeserving of success. All of that finally changed when I rediscovered that experience while doing personal development work as an adult and forgave myself and the others involved. I forgave the other kids for teasing and chiding me. I forgave myself for wetting my pants and making shameful, negative interpretations and beliefs as a result. I forgave the teacher for leaving my class in the library without thinking that someone might need to use the toilet. Even decades after the event had originally occurred, I was able to forgive the whole experience and release the unconscious burden I had long carried as an effect of it.]

So to forgive is to remove any negative judgments and disempowering interpretations and beliefs from events past. It is to make peace with the negative experiences of the past and release any limiting meanings and burdensome feelings so that you no longer allow them to affect your life. As you forgive yourself and other people involved in past time incidents and events, you can forgive and let go of entire experiences. Years or decades later, who did what to whom is really of little consequence. What *is* important is that you let go of negative meanings and beliefs created out of the past pain. In this way, you no longer allow the legacy of negative emotion and limitation from hurtful experiences of the past to control you in the present.

Forgive the Past, Live in the Present

Forgiveness isn't just limited to events and experiences of the past. Declining to attach any judgments and negative or disempowering meanings to events that happen to you in the present is also a form of forgiveness. By doing that – by choosing to keep your present experiences unencumbered of negative beliefs, interpretations and feelings – you ensure that you can move into the future in a more free, empowered way.

Finally, as you let go of the judgments, resentments and burdensome emotions from the past and as you decline to attach or hold onto any meanings about events, experiences or people from the present, you can live completely focused in this moment. You gain the ability to have your complete awareness and attention in the present, right here, right now. This is because you have no internal distractions and you're free of the baggage of guilt, anger, resentment or shame. There are no judgmental thoughts or uncomfortable, upsetting feelings silently gnawing at your mind to disturb your peace and detract from your awareness of the present moment. There's nothing to distract you from experiencing that innate sense of fascination with all that's available to explore, feel and do right here and now.

Now that you know more about what forgiveness *is*, in the coming chapters I'll share about *why* you should forgive, *how* to forgive and much, much more. This will include contemplations and exercises you can do and specific actions you can take. The first exercise is just below. And don't forget, for additional information, perspectives, exercises and support, you can always go to www.forgivenessclub.com.

Forgiveness Journaling Exercise – Chapter 1

Who or what do you need to forgive?

Make a list of people, incidents or experiences from your past or present that you need to forgive. Your list should include the people or situations you still hold some sort of negative judgments, feelings or thoughts toward or about. Very simply, include the people or situations, that when you think about them you experience agitation, tenseness, tightness, frustration, hatred, anger, resentment, blame, regret, guilt, shame, embarrassment or any other kind of discomfort or negative emotions. These kinds of judgments and feelings are indications that you have something to forgive.

Once you make the list of people or situations, then go back and write down what specifically needs to be forgiven. If you can't immediately think of a specific incident or circumstance, then stop trying to think; relax, breathe easily for a few moments and let your mind go still. Then focus on your heart and ask yourself, "What do I need to forgive with this person/situation?" Write down the first thing that comes to you, even if it doesn't make sense.

When you've finished the list take a break: you're done for now.

Chapter 2

Why Should I Forgive Someone Who Hurt Me?

Hanging onto resentment is letting someone you despise live rent-free in your head.
-Ann Landers

The question I'm addressing in this chapter is: "Why would I want to forgive someone who has hurt me, betrayed me, used me or treated me badly?" Why wouldn't you want to go ahead and continue to stay angry, resentful or blaming toward that person? Isn't it necessary to hold onto grudges and memories of your hurts to make sure it will never happen once more? Doesn't forgiving someone like that mean that they've won or even encourage them to hurt you or take advantage of you again in the future?

The Burden of Non-Forgiveness

If you haven't forgiven someone, you are carrying a burden. If you have someone or something that you've not forgiven, then you have a burden of anger, resentment, blame, guilt or shame. You're carrying around an emotional load that you don't need. It's an emotional load that will weigh you down and keep you from having the levels of joy and the kind of life that you really want to have. Perhaps more crucially, for as long you hold onto resentment, anger, judgments or blame against someone else, then you're firmly and negatively attached to that person.

Similar to what we did in the last chapter, let's again play a game of the imagination. This time we'll do it more quickly.

1. Take a moment and think about somebody that you still carry some anger, resentment or blame toward.

2. Pause and notice the kinds of feelings that accompany those judgmental, angry, blaming, resentful thoughts. Be aware exactly how those emotions feel in your body.

3. Does it feel good? Does it leave you feeling capable, energized and motivated? Or does it leave you feeling some other way?

I know for me it doesn't feel good; in fact, it's just the opposite. Bringing up old angry, resentful and blaming thoughts leaves me feeling heavy, tense, distracted. It robs me of energy and motivation to do what I need to do.

Bound Together

Another thing to consider is how easily you can become triggered about that situation or person. In the 1990's I owned and managed a litigation support services business for several years. There was an employee of mine, "Toby," who apparently built up feelings of anger and resentment toward me, until one day he blew up and quit in a rage. He confronted me while everyone else was around in the office and loudly proclaimed how he believed that I'd been unfair to him, should have promoted him, given him a raise and how I owed him. He accused me of all kinds of things that were from my perspective untrue and ridiculous. Then he stormed out of the office, leaving me and the other employees in shock. Soon thereafter, the shock of the incident wore off and I got upset. I felt resentful about what had happened and betrayed by him. I felt angry about the way that he'd yelled at me in front of the other employees, and accused me of all kinds of really nasty things.

For several years afterward, I dragged around a burden of anger, hatred, resentment and righteous indignation toward Toby. He was there every minute of every day living rent-free in my head. All it took for those old feelings to be triggered was for somebody that looked like him to walk by me. Or maybe I'd see a silhouette of someone in front of me at a theatre or store or even a photo somewhere that reminded me of him. Then I'd be right back in the past, reliving that old situation, experiencing those old upset feelings, the old judgments and the venomous, righteous anger.

That burden weighed heavily on me. I gave Toby a free ride around with me for far too long until I finally understood that I needed to forgive. Even though a part of me still felt like I had been right and that he had wronged me in that situation, I made a choice to go to work on forgiving him. With the decision and a little time, I did forgive and let it all go completely. Now I can see people who remind me of Toby and there's no negative trigger; there's no uncomfortable emotional reaction. I've evicted him from my head and freed myself of the burden of thoughts and emotions that had been my constant companion for far too long.

Why Should I Forgive Someone Who Hurt Me?

Emmet Fox, a renowned spiritual teacher of the early twentieth century, wrote once that our resentments bind us to the other person "with a cord stronger than steel." Think about that. When you're carrying resentment toward someone, you're actually bound to them. That's exactly what I was talking about a moment ago with Toby. When you're carrying the old thoughts, feelings and judgments around, something or someone can come along and remind you of the person you're holding resentment against. Then all of a sudden, that old situation with all of its upsetting emotions is right back in your awareness, tormenting you and distracting you from things that really need your attention and energy in the present. So a great reason to forgive is to get that person and incident out of your awareness and sever the negative connection you have with them. Then you can let go of the burden of anger and resentment so you don't have to carry it around any longer waiting to be ambushed by the negative thoughts and feelings.

Giving Up the Victim

Another reason to forgive somebody who has done wrong to you is so that you don't have to be a victim to the person or that situation any more. When you're holding onto resentment, and especially when you're holding onto judgments and blame, you're playing the victim. You're saying, "That person did it to me, I had no power over it, it's that person's fault." Blah, blah, blah. You get the picture.

Just think about what it feels like when you're a victim. Think about what it feels like when you're in a place of blaming and pointing your finger at someone else. It feels disempowering.

It feels like you have no control over your life. It doesn't feel good at all. Through forgiveness, you're able to take back your power. You're able to take back your responsibility and control over your own life. Most importantly, when you forgive, you reclaim your ability to create the kind of life that you want and deserve.

I should point out a couple things about victims and victimization before we move on. First, some people have adopted – even embraced – the victim role, using it as a primary life strategy. They have for some reason decided to view themselves and their circumstances from the perspective of the victim, believing that they are never at fault for anything "bad" that occurs in their lives. There is always someone else to blame for anything that happens to them or around them. For these people, playing the victim may be a way to gain attention and sympathy from others. It may be a way of trying to explain and rationalize things that they don't like, don't want or feel like they can't control. And it's certainly a way to avoid having to take responsibility for themselves and the situations and conditions of their lives. The people who live inside the role of victim perpetually see themselves as innocent of any mistakes, negligence, wrongdoing or inaction leading to a negative situation. They always have a quick excuse and justification for why they are not to blame and a finger ready to point at anyone or anything outside themselves as being culpable. They portray themselves as powerless over the events and circumstances of their lives, living completely at the effect of the world around them, rather than being at cause in any way.

Second, let me be clear that we all experience ourselves as victims in some way or another, because we all do get victimized by people and events in our lives. Whether the victimizing incidents were accidental or intentional, by the time we reach adulthood, every one of us has been hurt, betrayed, taken advantage of and otherwise victimized in innumerable ways. For some, the events and incidents are truly traumatic, abusive or life altering (I'll deal more with these kinds of "big events" in Chapter 8). I don't want to seem to minimize the effects of any victimizing incidents or the pain and loss that anyone has experienced. But there's an important distinction to make here. That is the distinction between being victimized by an incident and playing the role of victim in your life. You can be victimized somehow and still recover a strong sense of self. You can be hurt, wounded or suffer a great loss and still go on to live an empowered, self-responsible and fulfilling life. Alternately you can choose to see yourself as a perpetual victim, powerless to affect the world around you and frustrated by the raw deal life seems to continually give you.

You likely know someone who likes to play the victim, or you may even be that person to some extent. If this does describe you to any significant degree, then this book may not be for you. To get the real value available from this book, you have to be willing to give up being a perpetual victim. You must choose to begin taking responsibility for your own thoughts, beliefs, feelings and circumstances. But the good news is that there's hope and you have the ability to make a shift if you choose. This is where forgiveness comes in. Forgiveness gives you the opportunity to acknowledge ways in which you've been victimized, yet to step out of the victim role. Forgiveness allows you to take responsibility and reclaim your ability to create your life in a new, more empowered and much more satisfying way.

Reclaim Your Life-Force

Yet another reason to forgive becomes clear when you recognize and acknowledge how much of your energy goes into holding onto negative emotions and judgments. When you're holding onto resentment, when you're holding onto blame, you can actually feel the clenching and the tightness in your body. Take a moment to recall that feeling right now. In addition to the physical effort, you're also holding on emotionally and mentally, both consciously and unconsciously. You're expending your energy to do that – you're expending your precious energy to hate that person, to be resentful of or righteously judge that person. You're drawing on your finite and valuable supply of energy to blame and point your finger. In doing so, you're using this precious resource irresponsibly. You're further robbing yourself of your power, your control and your ability to create and live the life that you want.

So when you choose to forgive, take back your power, and decide not to play the victim any longer, you automatically gain access to all the energy that you've been wasting. You reclaim the energy that you've been dedicating to blaming, resenting and dragging around non-productive emotions. Once you do that, you can use your own energy once again to move forward and make a huge, positive difference in the quality of your own life.

Whether you're consciously aware of it or not, as long you have unresolved, unforgiven anger, resentment, blame and other negative emotions about some person or event, you're being weighed down. You're being robbed of some amount of your natural ability to be focused, clear, energetic and inspired in your life and activities. You're paying a high price to hold onto your negative judgments about people and experiences of the past.

Now consider:

1. Are those negative feelings – whether on a conscious or unconscious level – something that you want to be part of your daily reality?

2. Do you want to continue being negatively bound to the people and situations of your past, so that you're subject to being reminded of them unexpectedly and flooded with angry, blaming or regretful feelings?

3. Does it serve you to continue to play the victim to these people and situations of your past and to impose limitations on your ability to create, express yourself and enjoy life?

4. Can you afford to expend any of your valuable life force – your mental, emotional and physical energy – by holding on to and carrying around the burdens of the past?

5. Does it make sense to continue paying the price of refusing to forgive?

For any of the items above, I'd suggest the most empowering and freeing answer is "No."

These are among the most compelling reasons to forgive someone who has done you wrong. If you're ready for more insight into forgiveness and additional reasons to forgive, keep reading, there's more to come. In the meantime, if you want to begin to prepare for the forgiveness exercises yet to come, you can do the following short writing exercise. If that's not enough for now, then go to www.forgivenessclub.com to peruse all the material there.

Forgiveness Journaling Exercise – Chapter 2

How would your life be different if you were to forgive?

In order to want to forgive, you need to recognize the benefits to be gained through releasing the old mental, spiritual and emotional baggage you've been carrying. In this exercise you will envision yourself in your life having forgiven completely and set yourself free from the burdens of negative judgments, emotions thoughts and beliefs of the past.

Sit down with your journal or notebook, close your eyes for a few moments, breathe easily and relax. Then begin to imagine yourself going through your days free of the old judgments about yourself and others, liberated from old grudges, hurts and patterns of resentment, blame, anger or frustration and unencumbered by old feelings of guilt, shame or unworthiness.

How would your days be different? How would you feel about yourself and others without all that old stuff to influence your moods and interactions? What would your life be like if you were truly forgiven and free? What would you do differently? What would you replace all of that old stuff with? Imagine it all without any restriction. Let the thoughts, ideas and feelings come, and write about it until you're done.

Chapter 3

Why Forgive? Why Not Just Forget and Move On?

Forgiveness does not change the past, but it does enlarge the future.
-Paul Boese

A question I heard just the other day went something like this: "What's the purpose of forgiving anyway? I'd rather just forget about an incident and move on. Why would I even want to think again about something that was hurtful or difficult for me?" That's a great question, and to your mind it may seem to make a lot of sense.

So let's stop to consider it. Why should you or would you even think about a hurtful thing from the past and bring it up again? Why wouldn't you just forget about it and move on with your life? In response to that I say, to forget and move on is a great thing to do - if you can do it. And with awareness and intent you can do it for things that happen in the present. Unfortunately, for most of the situations of your past, you may have forgotten, but you probably haven't moved on cleanly and completely.

A Residue Lingers

I'm sure you've experienced that when you have something painful or hurtful occur, it stirs up a lot of "stuff." You encounter any number of thoughts, judgments and feelings about what has happened. You then have a short window of time in which to acknowledge, deal with and release all the "stuff" in a conscious, healthy way. That is, you have a relatively brief opportunity to intentionally forgive it. This is your window of opportunity to be able to truly forget it and move on. If you don't handle it in that conscious, healthy way and forgive it while it's still fresh, then things change. As time goes on, that "stuff" begins to settle down, your thoughts turn to other things, the feelings subside and the judgments fade into the background of your mind. But unfortunately the "stuff" doesn't just go away. Even though it may seem like you've forgotten and moved on from a hurtful experience, there's a residue that gets left behind. It's a residue from the emotions that were triggered, the judgments you had, and the meanings, interpretations and beliefs you made as a result of the experience.

Think about how easy it is to be reminded of an old painful, shameful or hurtful event from the past. You may just glimpse someone who looks like a person that hurt or betrayed you and all of a sudden old resentful feelings and thoughts come up to shatter your peace and prey on your mind. Or something may happen that reminds you of a time that you felt really shamed, guilty or humiliated. The memory triggers a physical and emotional reaction and you feel hot and flushed or sick and nauseated. You may even feel like you want to crawl into a hole somewhere and hide until the emotional reaction passes.

Have you ever had anything like that happen to you? It's obvious in these situations that you haven't really forgotten. Those kinds of responses are the result of that residue of judgment, feeling, thought and meaning that lingers still unprocessed and unforgiven in your internal world. So forgiving is the key to cleaning out all of the emotional, psychic and spiritual residue. When you forgive completely, then you've cleared the residue away; there's nothing left to negatively affect or limit you. Then you can truly forget and move on.

How the Residue Forms

As I mentioned in Chapter 1, when something happens to you that's hurtful, painful or traumatic, you make meanings and interpretations about it. As a human being, you're a meaning-making machine. You're hardwired to try to interpret and make sense of your experiences and incorporate them into a personal narrative or worldview. You might think of it as the story of your life: everything you tell yourself about who you are and why you are in your current circumstances. The meanings and interpretations you make about individual events aggregate and form into lasting beliefs. The beliefs weave together to shape your self-image and they determine how you see the world and how you interact with everyone around you. Meanings that you make as a result of emotionally painful incidents and events result in the formation of negative, limiting beliefs. These negative, limiting beliefs get mixed up with your judgmental thoughts and painful feelings to become the residue that lingers in your internal world.

This process of meaning-making and belief formation started for you at a very young age, yet it has left a lasting imprint on your life. From the moment you could begin to think and reason in even the most rudimentary ways, you began making meanings about your world. So by the time you were an adult, most of your core beliefs about yourself were already firmly in place. Your most limiting and disempowering beliefs were very likely formed early in your life, long before you had developed the rational capacity and defenses to understand and process painful events in more healthy ways. Your early experiences (especially those that were highly emotionally charged or physically painful or traumatic) laid the foundation upon which your current self-image is constructed. Though you might have forgotten the individual events and experiences, you have remembered and integrated their negative effects in into the very fabric of who you are.

The process of interpreting and meaning making continues throughout your entire life, typically below the level of your conscious awareness. If you want to become more conscious of the meaning making process, just pay attention to your internal dialog. Observe and notice that little voice in your head that provides a running commentary, evaluating, judging and categorizing everything you do and everyone you come into contact with. This voice and commentary is both the result and continuation of your personal meaning-making process.

A Meaningful Sunday

Here's an example of a painful (in this case shaming) experience I had and the negative meanings I made as a result.

When I was about four or five years old, one Sunday morning after service I was with another young boy in the basement level of our church. We were having a great time playing, running around and, as little boys tend to do, we were shouting to one another and making lots of noise. The minister's wife suddenly appeared, stopped us in our tracks and scolded us sternly for being disrespectful of "God's house." Her harsh tone and words made it clear that we were bad boys and should be ashamed of ourselves. One moment I was joyously expressing myself and having fun, and the next moment I felt completely crushed, deflated and shamed.

I took that run-in with the minister's wife and made it mean that I had been a naughty boy. I also made it mean that I'd offended God and that He was angry with me. As a result of this experience and other similar incidents that piled on top of it, I formed a belief that I was bad, shameful and that it wasn't okay to really express myself and have fun. Long after I'd forgotten this incident and well into my adult years, I was still affected by the residue of that event. I experienced it as a feeling of shame, guilt and a sense of impending disaster when I started to have "too much fun."

Finally, one day during a coaching process, I recalled that shaming incident. I saw how the meaning I had made and the corresponding belief had shaped my thoughts and actions, causing me to hold myself back and limit the amount of self-expression, joy and enthusiasm I could have. I was also able to recognize that the scolding wasn't really personal to me. The minister's wife had simply gotten some of *her* stuff stirred up by two boisterous, noisy, little boys and she had an emotional reaction. I was then able to let go of the negative judgments I had about her and forgive her for her part in the incident. I also forgave myself for making the negative meanings and limiting beliefs and for carrying them for so long. With forgiveness came the ability to release the old limitation and reclaim more of my natural exuberance and joy for life.

An important thing to note about the above story is that until I found the old negative meanings and beliefs, they were completely unconscious to me. I had long since forgotten the specific incident, and I had no understanding of how much it continued to affect me decades later. So while the idea of forgetting about a painful event and moving on sounds good in principle, in practice it can have some fundamental flaws. In the example above, I wasn't even aware of the negative meanings that resulted from the incident at the church. So there was no way for me to forget about it and move on because I'd done the forgetting part a long time ago. I just hadn't moved on; I was still carrying the residual effects of it with me every hour of every day deep below the surface of my conscious awareness.

Forgive, Then Forget

For events in the present, once you've forgiven by consciously acknowledging and dealing with any negative judgments or feelings, the "forget and move on" approach might serve you well. When there are no emotionally charged thoughts, meanings or beliefs left to carry forward with you, then forgetting is a great way to go. But you can't just decide to forget about all the painful events of your past and move on with your life if negative judgments, beliefs and feelings still remain - at either a conscious or unconscious level. They are the residue of past negative events that you need to deal with in order to free yourself to live a more joyful, productive life.

There are many ways in which the old residues of thoughts, judgments, feelings and beliefs can be exposed and the related incidents and experiences brought into your awareness to be forgiven. Perhaps the easiest and most effective is to simply monitor yourself, your moods and your emotions throughout the day. That is, you can decide to watch for your "stuff" to come up. Any time that you find yourself starting to feel agitated, upset, resentful, shameful, guilty, depressed or otherwise feeling bad – especially if it's for seemingly no apparent reason – you have a clue that the residue of some old incident or experience has gotten stirred up. Then rather than trying to stuff it down again, you can pay attention to it. Rather than trying to self-medicate with food, sweets, cigarettes, alcohol, exercise, sex or anything else that you use to manage your moods, you can be curious about it.

In these situations you can choose to investigate the source of your feelings so that you can forgive, forget for good and move on. When you get the chance, you can take a few moments to sit with the feelings and play emotional detective. As you consciously connect with and pay attention to the feelings, notice if any memories of past events or incidents start to come up. These would likely be things that you might not have thought about for a long time, or that you believed you were over. But if they come up for you in correlation with the uncomfortable or unwanted feelings, it means that they are still unresolved at some level. These would be incidents in which there is still someone or something you need to forgive. At the end of this chapter you'll find a journaling exercise designed to help you get to the hidden hurts that need to be forgiven from these incidents or experiences.

Forgiveness offers a method for clearing the emotional residue. It offers a means to release and let go judgments, negative attachments and limiting beliefs that form as a result of painful experiences. When you let go of the judgments and beliefs, then the past-time emotions are able to release and fall away. So in order to be able to move on cleanly and clearly, free of hidden emotional residue and limiting beliefs, it's important to forgive. It's important to acknowledge the emotions that may still be there, to find the judgments and beliefs that may be lurking in your conscious or unconscious mind and to let them all go.

You can forgive and forget an event or incident in the present and move on. Or you can forgive an experience from your past, thus reclaiming your ability to move on from it. Either way, before you forget you must let go of any negative judgments, feelings, meanings and beliefs in order to make sure that there's no residue to affect you, no baggage to drag around with you from the experience. However once you forgive, you don't have to forget. You may choose to forgive and remember, as I'll discuss in Chapter 7.

To summarize then, the purpose of forgiveness is to let go of the negative judgments and feelings, limiting interpretations or beliefs and anything else that might otherwise bind you to the hurts of the past. You forgive so that you can be clean mentally and emotionally, so that you can move forward in your life powerfully, with purpose, clarity and confidence. You forgive so that you can be free, fully self-expressed and have the ability to achieve your dreams. That's the true purpose of forgiveness and that's what we're going for.

I hope that this chapter has given you some new ways to think about forgiveness. I hope that it's maybe even brought up a memory of someone you need to forgive and that it's sparked within you a desire to let go of any negative emotional attachments and limiting beliefs that you might have.

Again, use the short exercise and questions below if you'd like some help with the process of identifying who or what you need to forgive. If you'd like a little more structure, download my free "Forgiveness Jump Start" kit from www.forgivenessclub.com/jump-start. It contains worksheets and a simple, step-by-step forgiveness exercise to help you get started. Or if you recognize that you need or want more support go to www.forgivenessclub.com/forgiveness-coaching for information on individual coaching and group processes. Regardless of what level of support you choose, do something. Then you'll be on your path to freedom from the negative judgments, emotional upsets, confining beliefs and any other residues of the past. Happy forgiving!

Forgiveness Journaling Exercise – Chapter 3

Finding the forgotten hurts that need to be forgiven.

This exercise is designed to help you discover things from your past that you don't recall or don't yet know need to be forgiven. These would have to do with experiences or incidents you may have forgotten about, or may believe are not important, but are still burdening you negatively or affecting you in some way.

When you find yourself feeling agitated, anxious, defensive, fearful, guilty, shameful or otherwise out of sorts for no apparent reason (especially if it's something that you have experienced in some repetitive manner), stop and choose to investigate the source of your feelings.

When you can, find a place to sit quietly for a few minutes, so that you can acknowledge, feel and journal about the feelings. Begin to ask yourself questions like: "What unresolved event or incident from the past might these feelings be connected with?" or "Who or what do I need to forgive in order to completely release and let go of these feelings?" Once you ask a question, just contemplate easily and let your mind wander for a few moments to see what comes up. Don't try hard to figure it out; instead let your unconscious mind present you with thoughts, images and connections.

Once you feel like some connection has been made, begin to journal and allow more recollections and thoughts to come out on the page. Then, write specifically about what is still unresolved until you've clarified who or what you need to forgive.

Chapter 4

When I Forgive, Doesn't That Condone the Other Person's Actions?

Forgiveness has nothing to do with absolving a criminal of his crime. It has everything to do with relieving oneself of the burden of being a victim - letting go of the pain and transforming oneself from victim to survivor.
-C.R. Strahan

One of the things that I hear a lot is some form of the question: "Doesn't forgiving someone mean that I'm condoning their actions or somehow making it all right that they hurt me?" I'm not sure why so many people believe that, but as I said, I get the question a lot. In fact, when I wrote a blog article on the subject of forgiveness recently, this very question was asked in one of the comments on the post. It was from a woman who said, "I have a hard time with forgiveness, because when I forgive an organization or a person, I feel like I'm condoning their actions and somehow making what they did to me okay."

Let's put that idea to rest right away: the answer is absolutely, unequivocally no. When you choose to forgive somebody for something that they did to you - whether it's something from the past or something in the present - you are absolutely not making it okay in any way that you were hurt or violated.

Forgiveness Is about You

Let's be very clear once again that forgiveness is really about you. It's about being responsible for yourself. You forgive for yourself first. You don't need to forgive for the sake of the other person at all. Now, I know that may seem a little strange at first glance. If it's the other person that hurt you, betrayed you or did something to you, how is it that by forgiving them you're taking responsibility and doing something for yourself?

We addressed this subject in Chapter 2 somewhat, but let's go a little deeper into it. You're ultimately responsible for the condition of your own life. When you forgive someone or something, you actually let go of a tremendous burden - the weight and stress of judgment, resentment, shame, blame, guilt or whatever it is that you've been holding on to. You let go of an emotional or energetic load that you've been carrying, sometimes for months, sometimes for years, sometimes even for decades.

There were a couple of big resentments that I dragged around with me for decades, and doing so exacted a high cost on me. It produced a tremendous amount of strain, emotionally and even physically. Holding onto the grudges drained my energy and hindered my ability to do and have what I wanted in my life. It prevented me from having more loving and connected relationships with family and others who are important to me.

When you forgive some person or organization, you need to do it with the intention of benefiting yourself first. The other party may also reap some benefit as a byproduct of your forgiveness. But that doesn't need to be your primary concern. Your biggest concern should be to take back your power and free yourself from the suffering and limitation that occurs as a result of holding onto negative judgments and feelings from the past. So don't worry: from this perspective, when you forgive someone, it does not condone their actions or make it okay that they hurt you. It's simply an act of releasing all of the negative, burdensome emotions and limiting beliefs that you've been holding about the situation.

No More Victim

Also as I mentioned in Chapter 2, when you forgive somebody it allows you to stop playing victim to the person or to the situation. It enables you to make the choice to reclaim your personal responsibility and take back your power. When you see yourself as a victim, then you'll naturally behave like a victim and make the kinds of choices a victim would make. When you *see* yourself as a victim, then you *are* a victim. But when you reclaim your responsibility, take back your power and forgive, you completely change the relationship. From a forgiven and clear place, the chances are good that you'll feel more empowered and that you'll be able to set better boundaries with that person or organization. You'll be able to interact with them in a new, more clear and powerful way that doesn't allow them to victimize you, hurt you or use you any longer.

When I Forgive, Doesn't That Condone the Other Person's Actions?

Forgiveness is about you first and foremost. It's not about making someone else right or wrong or changing someone else's perspective or understanding. It's about changing your mind about the past. Even if you did make someone realize they had harmed you in some way, you would still be casting yourself in the role of the victim. Ultimately, you can't control what other people do or think, and even if you could, it's what *you* think that matters. Making someone else wrong and judging them harshly will never make you feel better in the long term, because it just keeps you bound to the very people and events that caused you hurt in the past.

When you forgive someone, you're not condoning their actions; you're simply releasing the negative feelings, meanings and judgments you made about yourself or the other person as a result of their actions. You're freeing your mind from the negative memories about what they did to you so that there is no longer anything left there to trouble you. You're choosing to reclaim your power and you're choosing to become a completely new person in relation to them.

Forgiving the Past and the Passed

When you forgive, the person may not even know or care that you've forgiven them. In fact the person may be dead and long gone from this Earth. Several years ago, I realized that I needed to forgive my second grade teacher. I had finally been able to recognize the depth of the hurt and shame that I still carried from a series of incidents with her. I also knew she had likely long since passed away.

I'll call this teacher Miss Thompson, and at the time she was a big, physically imposing fifty-ish woman. As a young child I had a hard time staying focused in class and I was easily distracted. It took a lot of effort for me to pay attention and give sustained effort to assigned tasks and activities. Today it's likely I'd be tested and diagnosed with ADHD or something similar. But in the 1960's, that wasn't even a consideration; I was just one of the "difficult" students. I didn't perform well in class, and that frustrated Miss Thompson to no end. She knew I was smart because there were some things that I did brilliantly. But I tended to daydream, get distracted and not complete assignments so that overall, I consistently underachieved in my schoolwork.

I now suspect that Miss Thompson felt frustrated and unhappy in her own life, and that I and other "bad kids" in her classes provided an unfortunate but convenient outlet for those feelings. A few times during that school year, she got very angry with me for failing to finish an assignment or for not paying attention in class. On those occasions she came up to me, wrapped her large, strong hands around my little wrists and then lifted my small arms up off the desktop and slammed them down repeatedly, while verbally berating me. Bang, bang, bang, bang – over and over again until I was stinging and crying from a combination of the shock, the physical pain and the humiliation of being singled out and abused in front of my classmates.

When I realized that the negative feelings and beliefs from those experiences were still with me, I knew that I needed to forgive her. I don't condone her actions and I don't believe what she did to me was right. I didn't choose to forgive her because it was okay that she abused me and humiliated me in the classroom in front of the other students. I chose to forgive her because I no longer wanted to be burdened with the old hurt and limitations. I chose to give up the resentment, anger and blame that I had toward her. I chose to let go of the shame and feelings of unworthiness that I had taken on and dragged around with me for years. The act of forgiving her really had nothing to do with *her*; instead I was choosing to set *myself* free.

Freedom and Responsibility

And that's really what forgiveness is about. Forgiveness is about finding more freedom. Forgiveness is about taking full responsibility for yourself – not only for your past and your present, but for your future as well. Because when you forgive, you let go of the negative feelings and burdens of the past. As you do that, you're able to live fully present and engaged in the moment, with greater clarity and more of your own energy. When you're fully aware and engaged in the present, you're able to take definitive and decisive action to move forward in your life. You're able to work toward the fulfillment of your goals and desires in an empowered way, and enjoy the positive results of your choices and actions like never before.

Once again, does forgiving somebody else condone their actions or make it okay that they did something that hurt or victimized you? No, it doesn't. So don't ever let that notion stop you from making the choice to forgive and set yourself free. For a little different rendering of this topic, go to: www.forgivenessclub.com/forgiving-is-not-condoning.

Forgiveness Journaling Exercise – Chapter 4

What can you do right now to take back power and responsibility in your life?

In this exercise your goal is to make a positive change in your life right now by taking back some of your own responsibility. To do this, you'll identify places in your life where you are still playing the victim to someone or something, and then you'll choose to take back your power and do something different in at least one of the situations.

Start by making a list of people who you feel in any way victimized by, and whom you're still blaming for any conditions, situations or other facts of your life. (You can use your lists from the exercises in Chapters 1 and 3 as a good place to find these people or situations.) Then write down what specifically is wrong in your life that you currently blame them for. Be explicit and clear about the conditions or circumstances for which you make them responsible.

Once you've made this list, go through it and for each person or situation, answer the question: "If I weren't blaming this person/situation, what would I or could I do differently to change these circumstances?" Identify at least one specific action that you can take right now to take back your own responsibility and make a difference in your life. Then go do it and see what changes for you!

Chapter 5

When I Forgive, Doesn't That Let the Other Person Off the Hook?

Forgiveness in no way requires that you trust the one you forgive.
-W. Paul Young

In the last chapter I addressed the question: "If I forgive someone, doesn't that condone their actions, or make it okay that they hurt me?" And the answer is no, it doesn't.

The question I'm going to deal with here is a related one: "If I forgive someone, doesn't it mean that I'm letting them off the hook, or that I'm choosing not to hold them responsible or accountable for their actions?" Once again, the short answer is no. If you forgive a person or organization, it doesn't mean that you're letting them off the hook. If you forgive, it doesn't mean that you're letting them get away with what they did to you.

Bookkeeper Betrayal

Let me give an example. A number of years ago, in the small business I owned, I put a trusted employee in charge of the bookkeeping. It was a great relief to me to not have to deal with all of the details of the accounting and record keeping each week and it freed me up to give better service to my clients. But after a few months, this trusted employee got into my unlocked desk, went into the back of the company checkbook and stole some checks. Then over a period of a couple of weeks, he wrote checks against the account for his personal use and forged my signature on them. The amount of these stolen checks totaled several hundred dollars.

When I discovered what he had done, I was first extremely angry. Then I felt incredibly hurt and I couldn't believe that this man had betrayed my trust in that way. I fired him immediately, knowing that I would also hold him responsible for his actions. So after I fired him, I filed a police report to make sure that he was held legally accountable for what he'd done. In addition, I took action to ensure that he was held financially responsible for the theft and that he would repay the money he stole.

After taking those steps, I knew that I also needed to forgive him. In addition, I knew I needed to forgive myself for not being more careful and aware of what was happening. It was in the best interests of the business for me to find and hire another bookkeeper, yet I felt hesitant to do so. I realized that I needed to forgive and let go of the hurt emotions, the sense of betrayal and anger so that I could trust someone again. I needed to let go of my own shame and regret so that I could monitor the new bookkeeper without being driven by fear and suspicion to create an oppressive work situation by mistrusting and micromanaging them. I needed to forgive so that I could let it go and move on.

I *did* hold that employee responsible and accountable for his offense, for his betrayal of my trust and theft from the business. At the same time, I was able to use everything that was going on as part of the process of forgiving. By the time we were ready to work out a repayment schedule a few weeks later, I had already forgiven him for the betrayal and theft. I was able to engage in the situation in a non-emotional and matter of fact way, rather than being encumbered by feelings of hurt, anger and righteous judgment that could have caused me to behave in a blaming, punitive way and stalled the negotiations.

Let's be clear, though: in forgiving him it didn't mean that I took him back as an employee. It didn't mean that I gave him a letter of recommendation for future employers. I didn't let him back into my life socially or in other ways. I was clear that the relationship had changed. I didn't relieve him of the responsibility for his actions. But through forgiving, I was able to move forward in an informed and neutral way, not in a reactive, blaming or suspicious frame of mind. I set new boundaries and put new safeguards in place in my office. But I didn't have to continue to judge him, hold a grudge, stay in shame or feel fearful or defensive to do so.

Even if you're in a situation in which you don't have as much direct influence as I did, you can still forgive and you may still be able to hold the person accountable for their actions. It's true that I had ample recourse. I was the boss, I was able to fire the employee, report him to the police and hold him legally and financially responsible. But even if you're in a situation where you don't have as much power, you can still forgive. And when you forgive, you don't have to let the other person off the hook or refrain from holding them responsible for their actions.

When I Forgive, Doesn't That Let the Other Person Off the Hook?

Redefining Relationships

You forgive so you don't have to carry the burden of negative emotions and continue to play the victim. You also forgive so that you can be responsible for yourself, rather than trying to take responsibility for the actions and deeds of the other. At the same time, you can choose to conduct your relationship with the person that hurt you in a more responsible and empowered way. You can set boundaries, protect yourself from further hurt and make it clear they were in the wrong. But in doing so you don't have to take on the role of the victim.

Too many people simply don't understand the true purpose and power of forgiveness. Unfortunately, many have come to believe that to forgive someone else for an offense means that they'll be seen as a pushover or an easy mark for others. So these people end up remaining angry and defensive as a form of self-protection. On the other hand, I've also seen people who think that in order to forgive they have to meekly let perpetrators back into their lives with no consequences for the hurtful actions or no new boundaries in place to protect themselves. In either case, it's a real pity and there's no sensible reason for it. People in these situations are simply trapped inside a mistaken and misguided understanding of what it means to forgive.

I'd suggest that you can choose to forgive another in an empowered way. You can forgive and still set new boundaries, impose consequences and redefine your relationship to take care of yourself and your needs. I'd also assert that you if forgive and you reclaim your own power and personal responsibility in a situation, you can find ways of holding the other party accountable that you would not be able to recognize otherwise. You'll have options open up to you that would never be available if you continued to cling to a victim mentality, burdening yourself with anger, grudges or blame. You'll be able to take actions that you would never otherwise be able to take if you allowed your judgment to remain clouded by angry, negative judgments of the person or situation.

Punishment and Suffering

Many people I know feel like they have to remain angry and non-forgiving toward others in order to make a point. They feel like they're obligated to hold onto grudges to teach the other person a lesson or get some sort of revenge for being hurt. I know people who hold onto resentments and carry negative judgments in order to punish others. Still holding onto the hurt of a past situation, these people withdraw their love and approval, build up walls of protection and cut themselves off from those they blame for the hurts. Unable to let go, these people become cold in demeanor, condescending and judgmental in words and behavior. They often will even develop passively or overtly aggressive behaviors toward the ones they will not forgive. I see relationships of all sorts that have been crippled or destroyed by lingering resentment. I've seen and frequently heard of families, groups and organizations that have been ripped apart and turned into petty, vindictive, warring factions by non-forgiveness.

Maybe, like some of these people, you refuse to forgive and hold onto grudges because you believe that by doing so you'll somehow exact some sort of revenge on the person who hurt you. This kind of thing goes on frequently within families or

other close relationships. Many times it does feel like a form
of punishment for the person toward whom you're directing
your judgments and ire. But you also have to consider how
severely you're punishing and negatively affecting yourself.
When you hold onto anger, resentments and grudges in an
effort to get back at someone else, you're most clearly and
dearly hurting yourself. This too is a pity, for once again it
simply indicates a failure to understand the real point of
forgiveness.

By withholding love, affection and intimacy from someone
close to you, you're robbing yourself of the love, affection and
intimacy you could receive in return. With each negative
judgment you indulge you're also hardening your heart. With
every overtly or covertly aggressive word or action you're
digging yourself deeper into a pattern of mean-spiritedness and
vindictiveness. You're taking yourself a few steps further down
the path to becoming closed off and disconnected from those
you love, suffering in a bitter, lonely existence. Your
commitment to hold onto the hurts of the past and seek
revenge against those you blame will gradually separate you
from and drive away other family members and friends as well.
By steadfastly clinging to the role of victim and using it as
justification for lashing out at someone or something else, you
will ultimately become the victim of your own righteous
stubbornness and vengefulness. This doesn't even take into
consideration the costs you'll pay in terms of the burdensome
emotions, limiting beliefs, lost joy and diminished energy and
creativity. So again, you must ask yourself, "Is the price of
refusing to forgive worth it?"

Clifford B. Edwards

Responsibility and Accountability

It's not your responsibility to try to punish or "teach a lesson to" someone else for their deeds and misdeeds. It's supremely arrogant to think that you have the right to play judge, jury and avenger for the "crimes" of others. I operate from the perspective that everyone in this world is responsible for their own thoughts, words and actions. Absent some sort of severe psychological issue or neurological dysfunction, we all have to take responsibility for our choices and behaviors. I also choose to believe that ultimately everyone experiences the consequences of their own choices and actions in some form or another. So whether you believe in final judgment, or karma, or you just believe in the unconscious workings of the human psyche and the power of the conscience to somehow be that final arbiter, you can choose to believe that everyone will somehow, in some way be accountable for what they do. Even if you don't choose to believe that, it's still not your place to decide what's right or wrong and to take revenge. Your choices and actions are your responsibility; other people's choices and actions are their responsibility.

Once again, I have to emphasize that the focus of forgiving is on you and what you'll get out of it. You're the one who benefits through letting go of the negative thoughts, meanings and emotional burdens of a hurtful event. If you choose not to forgive because you want to somehow hold the other party accountable for their actions and try to punish them, you're withholding relief from yourself. You're simply perpetuating your own misery. Forgiveness is about you releasing your burden of anger, judgment, guilt or shame, resentment or blame and lightening your heart. It's about being able to reclaim your power so that you can be responsible for yourself and your actions. In doing so, forgiveness actually gives you the ability to consciously and intentionally create and live a happier, more fulfilling life. Forgiveness is *for* you and *about* you. Others may benefit as a result, but you're the one that you need to be most concerned about.

With that, I'll wrap it up for this topic. I love this question and I love talking about and discussing all things related to forgiveness. I'm pleased to share these perspectives so that you might start thinking about forgiveness in different, more useful and more empowering ways. The more you think about and consider the concepts of forgiveness, then the more likely you are to put them to use in your own life and to practice forgiveness. The more you and others put forgiveness into practice, the more peaceful our world will be.

Thanks for reading this far. Keep going, and practice a little bit of forgiveness each day. Remember, you can always get some additional support with forgiving by visiting www.forgivenessclub.com/forgiveness-coaching. Now, if you want to explore the concept of responsibility a little further, take some time to do the following writing exercise.

Forgiveness Journaling Exercise – Chapter 5

How are you trying to take responsibility for the actions of another?

The point of this exercise is to identify how and with whom in your life you're somehow punishing and therefore inappropriately trying to take responsibility for their actions, deeds or misdeeds. Then you'll have a chance to take action in at least one situation to make a change and do something differently.

Make a list of all the people you're holding some kind of grudge toward and whom you're either: 1) withholding affection, approval, intimacy or some other form of attention, or 2) actively trying to punish, get back at or "teach them a lesson" in some way (again, you can use names from your lists from the Chapter 1 or 3 exercises). For each of the people on the list, identify specifically what it is you're doing that indicates you're taking responsibility for them in some way.

After you list the people and how you're taking responsibility for them, then go back and for each, identify what the cost is for you in doing so. That is, what does it cost you in terms of resources – time, energy, money, things or other resources? Also include what it costs you emotionally. What do you lose in terms of your ability to give and receive love, affection, communication, connection or other emotional needs?

When I Forgive, Doesn't That Let the Other Person Off the Hook?

Once you've identified the costs, now go back through the list and (similar to the exercise in Chapter 4) determine one thing that you could do differently in each of these situations. What's one specific action you could take, or a specific behavior you could change to demonstrate your decision to give the responsibility for their actions or deeds back to them? Then pick at least one of the things you can change, and do it!

Chapter 6

How Do I Forgive?

Forgiveness is letting go of the past, and is therefore the means for correcting our misperceptions.
-Gerald Jampolsky

The purpose of this book is to bring more awareness and clarity to the topic of forgiveness. I often hear from people who are not clear on what forgiveness is or how they can actually do it. So in this chapter, I'm going to address the very basic question: "How can I or how do I forgive?"

Forgiveness Is a Choice

Many people these days seem to have the idea that they want to forgive or that they need to forgive, but they don't really know how to go about doing it. The first thing to be aware of in this regard is that forgiveness is a choice. Before anything else can happen, you must decide that you want to or that you're going to forgive. I've learned from my own experience and the experience of others that forgiveness often requires a commitment. In some situations, it can mean that you need to commit to a process or journey of forgiveness. Forgiveness can sometimes happen in an instant, it can take a little time, or it may require the longer journey or process. The amount of time needed to forgive completely usually depends on what kind of issue or experience you're working through and how honest and willing you allow yourself to be.

Forgiving Minor Events in the Moment

Many times, forgiveness can be done right in the moment as an event occurs or as soon as you realize that there's something to forgive. For example, I was driving on the freeway the other day, and another driver apparently was about to miss his exit. He suddenly veered across three lanes of traffic to get to the off ramp. As he did, he cut me off, surprising and frightening me; this triggered an immediate physical reaction of anger and fear in my body. But rather than getting caught in the upset, holding onto the anger, blaming the other person and creating a big internal drama about it, I made a choice to forgive. I took a deep breath to calm my body, acknowledging the fear and anger that had been triggered. Then as the emotion passed I told myself, "That guy didn't really see me. It wasn't personal and I don't need to make it mean anything."

With that I forgave him for being what I considered reckless; I forgave myself for getting so shocked and having an angry response and I let it go. In forgiving and letting go, I didn't have to carry all the feelings, upset and resentment with me for the rest of the afternoon. What I did in those few moments was to shift my perspective from one of the victim ("He did it to me") to a more neutral and empowered way of viewing it. I let go of the harsh, negative judgments that I had about him. In doing so, I was able to easily let go of the upset and feelings because there were no judgmental thoughts to hold them in place.

Now think about a time that something like this happened to you. Bring to mind an experience in which you had an emotional response triggered by some little incident that occurred. Maybe you righteously held onto your negative judgments and fed the upset with a repetitious internal dialog, and so it stayed with you for hours. It likely ruined a portion of your day by putting a big dark cloud over it and robbing you of joy, fun or other good feelings. You might have even complained about the little incident to someone else, making it an even bigger deal and dragging them into the morass of judgment and negativity with you. But it doesn't have to be that way. Any time a little incident like that occurs, you can simply choose to forgive in the moment and move on.

Forgiving After the Fact

Forgiveness can also be done at some point later, after an incident occurs. Many times, while you're in the middle of an experience, you may not even recognize or understand that you're in a situation that will hurt you or leave you feeling upset. Often, it's only later that you realize something hurtful has happened and you feel bad about it. In the recognition that you feel bad, you also have an opportunity to acknowledge that there's something you need to digest and forgive. In these situations, forgiveness once again starts with you making a conscious choice to let go. Then you do whatever is necessary to release the negative judgments that would cause you to hold on to any anger, resentment, shame or regret. Once you make the decision to forgive, you can use whatever specific technique works for you.

As I indicated earlier, one thing that I've found effective in letting go of negative judgments is to choose to see the incident or event in a new way. I consciously choose to shift my viewpoint on it. Sometimes all it takes is a simple decision to change my thoughts about it. Other times it's more effective for me to look for something that I can learn from the situation or find some way in which I have gained or can gain a benefit. In doing this I'm shifting out of the perspective that I've only been hurt or damaged by the experience. Though I may have felt hurt or pain at the time of the incident or event, I don't have to stay there as a victim to it. I can adopt the perspective that the experience will actually end up serving me in the long term. Once I can see and understand the larger gift or benefit of the situation, the negative judgments naturally and easily fall away. I'll give an example of how I've done this, then share a few specific techniques for shifting perspectives a little later in the chapter.

During college, I worked part-time at a little gas station not far from campus. It was the late 1970's and I was still young and quite naive. One Saturday afternoon, a guy came into the station, told me he was a friend of the manager, and fast-talked me out of $40 from the till as a "loan." In exchange, he gave me some collateral – a fancy-looking but ultimately worthless watch. Not long after he left, it occurred to me that I'd been conned. I first got angry at the guy, then I got angry at myself. I felt like a fool and was so embarrassed about my gullibility that I never told the station manager about having been fooled by the guy's story. Instead, I paid the money back out of my own pocket, even though it was a real stretch to do so.

I carried those negative feelings and judgments around with me for a long time and I felt victimized by the guy. I was so ashamed of having been so easily hoodwinked that I never told anyone about it. Then, several years later, someone tried to con me again – this time in a different setting and for a much larger sum of money. But guess what? Due to my earlier experience I was aware of the real intent of the fast-talking guy. I didn't go for it and saved myself some real financial pain. I had learned from the situation at the gas station to spot those kinds of scams. The guy back at the gas station had given me a $40 lesson in how to not get conned and I continue to benefit from that relatively small investment to this day.

Once I recognized what a valuable lesson that event taught me, I was able to let go of all my negative judgments, easily forgive myself and forgive the guy who conned me. So the key to forgiveness in this situation was for me to discover the real benefit of the incident and understand how it had helped me learn and grow as a person. I no longer see myself as having been victimized by it in any way and actually feel grateful for the experience. I take the perspective that the man was simply a teacher who came to share a lesson that I'd need later in life.

What about the Really Big Events?

Sometimes there are big events that occur, experiences that are life changing and maybe even life shattering. These are the kinds of incidents and experiences that feel really traumatic and that can potentially impact you negatively in significant ways for years or even decades. They often involve a major loss of some sort – personal, emotional, physical, financial or other loss. These experiences may require a process of grieving and healing of the trauma before you're ready to forgive. These life-changing events may need to be digested and forgiven over a period of time or as part of a journey. But once again, it has to start with a choice to forgive and move on. The point of this kind of journey of forgiveness is to get to a place where you have surrendered all of the righteous judgments, shame, guilt, anger, blame, regret, resentment or anything else that burdens you. The journey ends when you can completely give up the victim role and release any lingering feelings of limitation or restriction in your life.

As you process through it all you can once again look for the life lesson or benefit that the painful incident has provided. Doing so will help release the grip of negative judgments, emotions and beliefs. You can open your mind and heart to begin to reinterpret the experience and view it as something that has ultimately given you gifts and prompted you to evolve. Alternatively, you can cling to the perspective of a victim, and see it as something that was only negative and damaging to you. You get to choose.

The old cliché says that "every dark cloud has a silver lining." Based on my own experience and that of thousands of others I've interacted with over the years, that old adage is true. I would now assert that every major life event that is hurtful or negative at the time it occurs actually comes bearing the seeds of a truly magnificent gift. These experiences challenge you to grow in ways that you never would have otherwise. They open the doors to new opportunities that would have otherwise remained permanently closed to you. Forgiveness happens easily when you can see, understand and embrace the value and benefit of the painful events of your past or present.

How to Forgive

In terms of the "how to" of forgiveness, there are many different techniques. Some are very simple, like the one I described in the section above: "Forgiving Minor Events in the Moment." You just make a choice to forgive, acknowledge the emotions and feelings and let them go. You consciously decide to shift your perspective and to release judgments, negative feelings and victimizing interpretations when something happens. You can also say to yourself, "Oh, I don't need to get upset about this. I don't need to turn this small incident into a big thing that ruins my whole day." You deliberately choose forgiveness instead of clinging tightly to the hurt or grievance, whether it's toward yourself or another.

When it comes to forgiving after the fact, there are many techniques too. To re-emphasize, the key to forgiveness is in your willingness to soften your heart and your ability to let go of the negative judgments you've held about the event or experience. It's when you decide that you're no longer willing to be the victim of the situation and you're ready to move on from the drama and emotion of it. You can let go of the negative judgments and move on by shifting your perspective and seeing the incident, circumstance and/or perpetrator in a new way.

Some More Simple Techniques for Shifting Perspectives

Journaling or List-Making Exercises:

1   Write a forgiveness letter to the person, people or group that hurt you. Write out anything and everything that you would want to say to them in order to express your

feelings, to release your judgments, to reclaim your responsibility and power, and to forgive, let go of the baggage and be clean, clear and complete with them. Note that this letter can be written to anyone living or dead, and can be, but does not *need* to be sent to them. (For a step-by-step guide to writing a forgiveness letter to someone else, go to www.forgivenessclub.com/forgiveness-support.)

2   Sit down and write or journal about the hurtful experience, expressing on paper the feelings, emotions, meanings and interpretations that it holds for you. Follow up by examining the experience to look for the benefits of it and claim in writing every possible lesson or bit of wisdom you can find for yourself within it. (At the end of Chapter 7, you'll find a journaling exercise to help you do this.)

3   Make a list of all the good things that you've gotten in other ways from your relationship or association with the person or organization up to this point. This is especially effective when forgiving someone close to you like a family member, friend, colleague or an organization you belong or have belonged to. For example with a friend this list might include the friendship, mutual support, fun times and activities you've experienced together. When you "count your blessings," recognizing the wide range of positive things you've received and acknowledging the value of the relationship, it's much easier to let go of the negative judgments and feelings.

4   Imagine seeing the world through the eyes of the other person, experiencing what it would be like to be them. Write about the incident or events from their perspective describing the fear, pain, stress, anxiety, insecurity or other difficult circumstances that might have driven them to

behave in the way they did. Continue from their viewpoint by writing about any guilt, shame, regret or remorse that they may still be feeling about their choices and actions in the situation that hurt you. The purpose of this exercise is to help you shift your perspective out of that of the victim, and into one of compassionate understanding of the physical, mental and emotional factors that may have contributed to their upsetting actions or hurtful behavior.

Prayerful or Meditative Practices

1 Set aside ten to fifteen minutes to sit quietly while tuning into feelings of humility, acceptance and compassion. As you connect with the feelings, begin to repeatedly offer a mental statement of forgiveness. At the same time, see yourself as loving, powerful and whole and send thoughts of love and blessing to the person or situation. Do this exercise for as many days in a row as needed, until you feel a shift in your thoughts and attitudes towards the person or situation and a sense of release.

2 Similarly, make a daily practice for a time of offering prayer or positive affirmations for the other party to have great success, to receive and be blessed by everything they want and need. When you consciously bless them, wish them well and hold them in a positive light, you naturally loosen the grip of the negative judgments, emotions and beliefs related to the person or incident.

3 For some people, the act of praying to a Higher Power for help in forgiveness is useful. These prayers can include any or all of the following elements.

A. Declaration of your intention and desire to forgive and be free.

B. Request for help in gaining the understanding and insight needed to see the situation in a new way.

C. Request for support in releasing the judgments and hurt feelings.

D. Imagining an actual turning over of the burdens of negative judgments, emotions, thoughts and beliefs to the Higher Power.

E. Statements of acceptance, compassion and forgiveness.

F. Offering thanks and gratitude in advance for the freedom and blessings of having forgiven.

G. Anything else that helps you feel more accepting, forgiving, compassionate, empowered and free.

4   Others recommend using repetition of a statement of forgiveness, either verbally or in writing as a way to release burdensome judgments and emotions. You can do this in order to help forgive others or yourself. For some, this means a literal interpretation of a biblical teaching from the book of Matthew, to forgive seventy times seven. For example, writing seventy times seven (490) times, "I forgive _____ for _____." Or stating the same thing aloud over and over 490 times and repeating for a period of days or weeks as needed.

Just Choose Forgiveness

If none of the methods I've shared above resonate with you or seem to make sense to you, there are many more methods and ways to forgive. There are far more than I can possibly try to name and explain in this short chapter. But with a little research online, or in your favorite bookstore, you can come up with a technique that works for you. You can also go to my website, www.forgivenessclub.com to read articles, watch videos and learn more about forgiveness in a variety of ways. At the end of this chapter, I've also included links to a few additional online resources for information about forgiveness.

The most important thing is that you find something that's appropriate for you and the particular circumstance that you have to forgive. Any method is fine as long as it works and is safe and healthy for you. You'll know that the forgiveness technique works if it brings you to a place of true release, relief and peace allowing you to reclaim your power and responsibility. It doesn't matter whether you use a practice or method that I've suggested or find something elsewhere. What does matter is that you do forgive and set yourself free.

I want you to know that no matter what kind of painful, hurtful or unresolved experience you have in your past, you can make a choice to forgive and set yourself free. If you choose and commit to forgiving, you will be able to get to a place of being clean and clear with any incident and set yourself free – free of the burdens of the past, free of any resentment, free of any anger or blame, free of any guilt, regret or shame. Forgiveness is a path to ultimate freedom and freedom gives you the ability to choose and create the future that you want.

Additional Forgiveness Resources

http://www.forgivenessweb.com/

http://theforgivenessproject.com/

http://www.thepowerofforgiveness.com/resources/

http://www.radicalforgiveness.com

Forgiveness Journaling Exercise – Chapter 6

What new perspectives can you take to help you let go of negative judgments?

For anything that happens in your life – and in the world at large – there are a multitude of different perspectives from which you can view and interpret it. The point of this exercise is for you to practice perspective-hopping. You will revisit some of the hurtful, painful or limiting incidents or events from your past, and choose to see them in new ways. In changing your perspectives, you'll find there are ways of interpreting the situations so that you no longer have to judge them as bad, wrong, hurtful or whatever. When you are able to give up your negative judgments about an incident or event, then you automatically open the door to being able to forgive.

Select three to five things from your list of incidents or experiences that you need to forgive (from exercise in Chapter 1) and write them on a new journal page. Select a few that you consider to be smaller or less significant incidents and then add one bigger, more significant, hurtful event. As you look through the list, recognize that you're still viewing these from the perspective that you were somehow hurt, diminished, limited or otherwise damaged by the experiences. Acknowledge as well, that there are many other ways in which you can view and interpret them.

Decide to make it a game and to challenge yourself to come up with multiple alternate perspectives from which you can view the events. Start with the smaller ones and work your way to the most significant one. Especially focus on finding points of view that allow you to feel more empowered and responsible, to be okay with and maybe even amused about the incidents. Write down as many different perspectives as you can think of even if they initially seem silly, irresponsible, nonsensical or bizarre. As you write down the various viewpoints, also describe briefly how you could feel and act differently from within each.

Remember, the purpose of doing this is to demonstrate that a myriad of perspectives always exist and none of them is inherently more true or right than another. When it comes to perspectives and interpretations, you get to choose. Since once upon a time you chose the old point of view and all of the judgments that come with it, you can now decide to choose something new and let the judgments go.

Chapter 7

I Want to Forgive, but Do I Have to Forget?

The stupid neither forgive nor forget; the naive forgive and forget; the wise forgive but do not forget.
-Thomas Stephen Szasz

The question for this chapter is based on a common saying, something that you've probably heard hundreds of times in your life. "Forgive and forget" is how it goes. "You've got to forgive and forget." But is that true? Further, is it even a good idea? In an earlier chapter I answered the question: "Why forgive? Why not just forget and move on?" You'll find here a different take on the whole notion of forgetting.

So the question I'll address here is: "I want to forgive, but do I really have to forget?" I'm going to cut out the suspense and get right to the short version of the answer: no. When you forgive, you don't have to forget. In fact, in most cases, it will actually be beneficial to you to forgive and remember.

Hurtful Events Happen

There are lots of things that happen to us every day, month and year of our lives. Many of those experiences feel difficult, are somehow hurtful and cause physical, emotional or psychological pain. These are the things that we need to forgive and let go of in order to have as much freedom, clarity, flexibility and creativity as possible. Because it's these painful experiences around which we tend to generate negative meanings and judgments. The negative meanings and judgments then lead to emotional burdens and many different forms of limiting thoughts, beliefs and habits.

Some of the painful incidents are pretty minor and insignificant in the larger context of our lives. These are things that we can easily forgive, then forget them and move on. For example, I was walking through the Chicago airport just a couple of days ago and experienced a hurtful incident. Another guy was on his phone, distracted by the conversation and banged into my leg with a big piece of rolling luggage. In the moment that it happened, it was painful and I immediately felt some anger come up. I began judging the guy and mentally berating him for being so careless. I was all primed to wind myself up into a rant about how I hate airports and the stupid, inconsiderate people that seem to populate them. Then I caught myself and took a breath.

I knew that it was just an accident; it wasn't a personal or premeditated attack on me. I also had to admit that I've been guilty of being distracted, careless and inconsiderate myself. So I made a quick decision to forgive the person and the incident then let go of the judgments and upset. I chose to let it go and move on rather than raise my stress levels, continue to grumble and make the rest of the walk to my departure gate unpleasant. It wasn't really a significant event. If I hadn't used it as an example here, I wouldn't remember this incident at all in a few more days, let alone months or years from now. It's something that once forgiven, I can easily forget about for good. The real issues here are effect and intention: the event had little or no long-term effect on me (I wasn't injured, I didn't miss my plane) and the person had no intention of hurting me. But what about times when the effect *is* more long-lasting or there *is* intent to harm?

Painfully Significant Experiences

There are other incidents and experiences that have a lot more significance and more emotional charge. These are things that may be accidental but have long lasting, negative effects. Or they are offenses that have been committed against us by others intentionally or even maliciously. All of us have had really dramatic or traumatic things happen to us, events that alter the course of our lives forever. As we'll discuss in more detail in Chapter 8, these are the painful events or incidents that may require some time and support to process through, forgive and let go. But these are also the experiences that serve as real life lessons. They come offering the greatest potential for wisdom and the most opportunities for personal growth and evolution. These are the experiences that we don't want to forget, and they are also the ones that are most important to forgive.

When you forgive, what you're doing is choosing to forget and escape the influence of negative judgments limiting thoughts, beliefs and fears that you might have taken on as a result of an experience. You're releasing and forgetting the lingering feelings of hurt, anger, shame, guilt, regret or blame you might have been holding onto. Yet again, in every experience of your life there's something to be learned. Especially the painfully significant events that have shaken you up or affected you deeply: these have valuable lessons, gifts and insights to offer if you choose to seek out the wisdom. They have the ability to equip you to move forward more effectively in your life, with greater confidence, maturity, understanding and compassion.

A Painful Personal Lesson

For example, many years ago in my first real relationship with a woman, I was wildly infatuated and supposed that I'd found true love. But I was completely inexperienced in relationships and didn't know how to behave in one. I mistakenly thought that I had to try to change myself to match her preferences and desires. I thought I needed to mold myself to be someone that she would want instead of just being me, because I didn't believe that the authentic me was enough. I also didn't know how to communicate well, so in trying to please her I hid my true thoughts and feelings – especially if I thought they would diminish me in her eyes. As a result, I was guarded and closed down emotionally. I tended to take it personally when she'd express even minor dislikes or criticisms about me. That reinforced the belief that I needed to change, put me even more on guard and prevented me from responding in constructive ways to her feelings and opinions.

Within about three months, she broke up with me saying that we didn't have the right chemistry. It was my first breakup experience and I was devastated. I felt like a failure; I'd been rejected and it reinforced my old belief that there was something wrong with me. I also felt shamed, angry and regretful. It left me feeling depressed, defeated and searching for answers as to why it had happened to me when I'd tried so hard to please her.

But ultimately I gained from the hurt and devastation. As I was able to digest the experience and get input from others, I had the opportunity to learn more about myself and more about relationships. I learned that I could have more trust and confidence in myself. I came to understand that I didn't need to try to become a different person in order to be successful in a relationship. I learned that I needed share and communicate more openly; I needed to be present and listen closely to my partner while talking, rather than listening to the dialog in my own head. It taught me that the breakup of a relationship isn't necessarily personal (although it usually feels that way). Surviving and growing from the experience gave me the courage to go into the world of love and intimacy again and then again and again, to eventually meet the woman who is now my wife of twenty-two years.

Find the Lessons, Apply the Wisdom

So that first breakup - though it felt so excruciatingly painful at the time – contained many valuable lessons. Once I could see all that it had helped to teach me and how it had prompted me to grow and mature, I came to view it with new eyes. With the benefit of compassion and wisdom gained, I no longer harshly judged either the woman or myself for the roles we played in it. I forgave myself for being so naïve, so expectant and for setting myself up to be hurt. I also forgave her for not wanting to be with me and breaking my heart. Looking back, I now feel grateful to her for the learning experiences she provided. I was able to take the lessons of that first abbreviated relationship and apply them to my next relationship, and the next after that and so on. Then I was also able to use my experiences in each of those to continue to grow and gain wisdom that has proven useful to me in my marriage as well as in other relationships in my life.

When you make the effort to extract the lesson, gift or wisdom from a painful event and put it to use in your life, something shifts inside you emotionally. It makes forgiveness easier – almost automatic – for you can then understand the hurtful event as actually having contributed something positive and useful. When you can see the experience as something that has benefited you and has helped you move forward in your life, then there's no cause to try to forget it. When you really understand the value that a painful incident has given and continues to deliver, you can let go of all your negative judgments and look back on it with appreciation rather than resentment, regret or shame. You can remember the event as a blessing, and feel gratitude for the wisdom you've gained rather than wishing you could forget the hurt and unresolved feelings. In the moment you can recall it with gratitude you have integrated the gifts and lessons of the experience and know that it's forgiven.

Change Your Past, Change Your Future

Adopting this perspective and engaging in the kind of honest self-reflection it requires offers you the opportunity to change both your past and your future for the better. This is the real value of not forgetting. Let's be clear: unless you have a time machine, you won't be able to change the facts of what happened to you in the past. Unfortunately, the laws of physics seem to preclude building a time machine, so the best option remaining is to change the way that you remember. Through mining hurtful experiences for the value and benefits they hold, you change your interpretations and understandings of them and therefore change how you remember them. You shift the quality of your memories from negative to positive and you alter the story you tell yourself and others about your past. You can change your perceptions about anything that has happened to you in the past, and in changing your perceptions, you change your current reality.

When you're able to recognize and embrace the lessons available to you from past hurtful experiences, you gain access to the benefits those experiences hold for you in the present and the future. When you extract and remember the knowledge and wisdom acquired, you have the ability to consciously and intentionally apply it in your current and future circumstances to improve the quality of your decisions, your results and your life.

So when you forgive do you have to forget? No, you don't. In fact, the more significant the event, the more likely that it will be valuable for you to remember the experience and what you've learned from it. You can remember the wisdom, lessons and value as you forget and let go of the negative judgments, painful emotions, disempowering meanings and limiting beliefs. You will gain all the benefits and positively affect both your perceptions of the past and your ability to create a better future. More importantly, you'll set yourself free from upsetting thoughts and judgments, lingering pain and burdensome beliefs.

So I invite you to adopt the practice of examining the hurtful experiences of your life – past and present – for the potential lessons and value that they contain. As you do, you'll find that you're able to forgive and move on more quickly and easily. Then, rather than forgive and forget, you can forgive and remember to your continuing benefit. For help with finding the lessons and wisdom of past events, I've included a special exercise below. For additional ideas and support, go to www.forgivenessclub.com/forgiveness-support.

Forgiveness Journaling Exercise – Chapter 7

What value and benefit can you extract from a painful experience of the past?

The purpose of this exercise is to examine a hurtful experience to look for and claim every possible lesson or benefit you can find for yourself within it. When you're able to find the value that an experience has to offer or has already given you, then it's much easier to allow the feelings of hurt and judgments to drop away so that you can forgive.

Sit down with your journal or notebook in a quiet place. Bring to mind one of the more painful or even traumatic incidents that you've identified from your past. Pick one that still feels unresolved or has some emotional charge attached to it. As you do, take a few moments to breathe and relax your body.

Once you feel relaxed and calm, imagine stepping out of the emotions and judgments you have about the situation so that you can view it from a perspective that is objective and neutral.

Now, with an intention to find some kind of benefit or value, consider that there are ways in which you've grown and changed for the positive as a result of the incident. It's helpful to think of the experience as having been a catalyst for change that has set you on a different course in life in some way. (Just like the example of my first relationship above, the painful breakup ultimately led me to grow, evolve and find a more fulfilling, long-lasting love.)

Allow ideas and thoughts about lessons that you've learned from the experience to begin to come to you and write them down. Become aware of ways in which you've developed positive or useful personal qualities or characteristics. Recognize things that you've done or achieved as a response to the experience that you wouldn't have otherwise. See that perhaps it has given you more wisdom and understanding or an enhanced ability to be helpful and compassionate with others. How much positive change, value or wisdom has come to you directly or indirectly as a result of that painful event of the past?

Continue writing until you feel a shift occur - an emotional shift in how you now see, understand and feel about the experience. Breathe, relax and acknowledge your new insights and perspectives, letting them integrate into your view of the past. Do you now feel a little more open to forgiving yourself or any others involved in the incident?

Chapter 8

How Do I Know If Something Is Too Big to Forgive?

Forgiveness is an act of the will, and the will can function regardless of the temperature of the heart.
-*Corrie Ten Boom*

The question I'm addressing in this chapter is a follow up to that of Chapter 6: "How Do I Forgive?" It's an important one for many people, especially those who have been betrayed in a major way, suffered really traumatic events in their lives, or who have been the victim of ongoing abuse of some sort. The question is:: "How do I know if something is too much or too big to forgive?"

Well, let me give a quick answer to that question right off the bat. There is *never* anything that is too much or too big to forgive. As humans, we have an amazing capacity for resilience, adaptation to circumstances and evolution. We have a huge capacity for learning and growth as individuals. We also have the ability to seek and find levels of compassion, understanding and support that will allow us to open our minds to new perspectives and our hearts to unfathomable depths of love and acceptance. So when we choose to forgive, when we make a conscious decision to make peace and let go of the burdens and bondage of the past, we can always find a way.

Big Hurts Happen

Some hurtful, life-altering experiences are the result of a single event. Some big hurts build up over time due to an accumulation of smaller incidents or events. As a result of either of these kinds of experiences, you can end up carrying righteous judgments and holding onto blame, resentment and hatred toward a person or organization. You can also end up carrying around a burdensome load of pain, shame, guilt, anger and other unresolved feelings. The experiences can leave a thick emotional residue that diminishes or limits you – and it can feel like something that will exist within you and affect you permanently. This emotional residue mixes with the load of negative meanings, judgments and beliefs you hold about yourself and others, to form a noxious glue that bonds you firmly to the past.

But the good news is that forgiveness is a choice. I'll say it again: when you consciously choose to forgive, and do so with purpose and determination, there's always a way to set yourself free. As I've emphasized so many times in this book already, the most important thing to understand is that forgiveness is really about you and your freedom. When you consider the prospect of trying to forgive someone else for the hurtful, damaging or traumatic experiences they brought into your life, it can look like an overwhelming task. The intensity of the anger, resentments or grudges may feel too big to work through or let go of. It might seem that what someone did to you is unforgivable - too much or too big to ever make peace with, let go and forgive.

A Battering Betrayal

Angela is one of the most joyous, optimistic and passionate people I know. She feels completely in tune with her life purpose, expressing herself through singing, coaching, leading and inspiring others. She's married to the love of her life, has a strong, supportive network of family and friends and considers herself to be fabulously blessed in the ways that matter most. Angela shines as a bright light and example of happiness, fulfillment and contribution.

Things weren't always this way for Angela. I first met her several years ago as a student in a coaching training class I helped to lead. At the time she was slogging through the painful process of rebuilding her life in the wake of a devastating divorce. The divorce came as a result of an incident that many people might deem unforgivable. A year earlier, Angela's husband of twenty years had announced that he was leaving her for another woman. Michael's abrupt decision to end their seemingly good, solid and loving marriage caught Angela completely off guard. He had given no indications that he was unhappy, and in fact the relationship had seemed better than ever in the couple of years just prior. Needless to say, she was left feeling stunned, betrayed and lost in a swirl of questions. "Why now? What happened? How could you? What's wrong with me? What will I do now? How can I face my family and friends? How will I survive?" These questions and myriad more gnawed at her mercilessly day and night.

The Despair of Wasted Years

Perhaps worst of all, it was only after her husband left that Angela realized her entire life had been constructed around what he wished to do and accomplish. For two decades she had selflessly ignored her own desires and worked to help make Michael's dreams come true. All that remained for her was a home, a business and way of life that she'd never really wanted – other than because it was what he had wanted.

On the heels of this recognition, Angela pummeled herself brutally with self-recriminations for wasting twenty years of her life. She thrashed about in the searing heat of rage and humiliation of having been scorned. At the same time, she was virtually paralyzed by the overwhelming combination of loss, shame, guilt, fear and much, much more. For weeks, Angela barely left her house, sneaking out only late at night to get only what she needed to survive. She did everything possible to avoid the knowing glances and inevitable words of pity, condescension or judgment from other members of her small, close-knit community. Further, having come from a deeply religious family in which divorce for any reason was unthinkable, Angela was even too ashamed to reach out for the love and support of those closest to her. She felt abandoned, alone and that she had lost her purpose and will to live.

Hope and a Clear Decision

During the first excruciating months after Michael left, Angela saw no hope for the future and could not conceive how she would ever be able to forgive and to be okay again. She had experienced the most devastating, life-altering betrayal that she could have imagined. But little by little she began to catch glimmers of hope. During one of the glimmers, she made a conscious decision that she must find a way to forgive. Drawing on the strength of her religious faith, she knew she must find a way to let go of the heavy burden of resentment, blame, anger and hatred toward Michael and the other woman. With a desire to heal and commitment to move on with her life, Angela decided that she must somehow let go of her judgments, recriminations and shame.

In making that decision - consciously and deliberately - something began to shift for Angela. At a local bookstore she happened upon a book called *Spiritual Divorce - Divorce as a Catalyst for an Extraordinary Life* by Debbie Ford. She devoured the book, allowing herself to be nourished by its message of empowerment, responsibility and hope. Inspired by the book, Angela worked up the courage to ask for help - something that she'd never given herself permission to do before. She hired a Spiritual Divorce Coach to take her through a step-by-step process of healing her shattered heart. She began to see new possibilities for her life and new doors began to open to her.

Forgiveness as a Process

Over a period of months, Angela worked through her personal darkness and fears. After receiving the support of a coach, she made the decision to join a coaching training program and learn how to support herself and others in a similar way. Most importantly during this time, Angela began to understand the true gift of Michael's decision to leave. She found herself becoming an entirely new person, with a new, more fulfilling life opening up before her. She knew that this was a life she'd never have been able to experience within the comfort and secure familiarity of her marriage with Michael. Angela came to understand that he had to leave in order for her to stretch and grow into a more soul-satisfying future. With that realization, she was able to shift perspective. She let go of the judgments and allowed the feelings of anger and resentment to transform into gratitude and relief. Angela was able to let go of the recriminations and negatively charged emotional burdens of the past so that she could forgive Michael and the other woman fully.

Angela knew that she had forgiven completely when she volunteered to make the wedding cake for Michael and his new bride. Now a few years later, Angela has met and married a man she considers to be *her* soul-mate. They have become close friends with Michael and his new wife, both of whom participated in Angela's wedding as well. They all now share in open, caring and supportive relationships with each one another. They live completely unencumbered by judgments, resentments, blames or anything else that might be dredged up from the past. Their local newspaper even did a short feature article on the amazing story of forgiveness and reconciliation. (See article here: http://goo.gl/TfZdb.)

The Power of Choice

Things might have been much different for Angela and Michael. Like so many other millions of rejected spouses, Angela might have chosen to hold onto her hatred, blame and resentment. She might have felt entitled to nurture the simmering anger for years or decades. Angela might have allowed it to eat away at her, turning her into the perpetual victim of an ex-partner years removed from her daily life. In choosing to hold on, she would have robbed herself of any chance for true happiness. But instead Angela made the choice to forgive. As unnatural as that choice felt, as non-intuitive as it might have seemed from inside the haze of painful emotions, she somehow knew it was what she needed to do.

At the time Michael left, the shock of the betrayal was enormous, even seemingly insurmountable for Angela. Initially it may have felt unforgivable to her. As time went on it might have felt good to hold a grudge, to righteously judge Michael and his new wife for their transgressions against her. It would have been easy and convenient to wallow in the hurt, pain and self-pity, blaming them for ruining her life. It could have happened that Angela would spend the remainder of her years alone, feeling bitter, resentful and mistrusting of love. But Angela chose a more difficult, more courageous path. She chose to demonstrate love and caring for herself, by forgiving them.

As Angela will freely admit, the process of coming to complete forgiveness wasn't quick and it wasn't easy. It was a journey – at times blissfully hopeful and at times wrenchingly scary – that had to be completed one determined step at a time. And she will now tell you with absolute conviction and belief that her divorce as the best thing that ever happened to her. It didn't have to be that way, but it was. Angela could have stubbornly clung to the belief that Michael had irreparably damaged her when he left. She could have collected lots of evidence to justify why that was true. She could have continued to live as a perpetual victim of the circumstances of the past, rather than creating a new and better life in the present. So when Angela chose to forgive, she was the one who ultimately benefited the most. Forgiveness gave Angela the key to a new reality and the fulfillment of her hearts deepest desires now and into the future.

Angela's story is just one small example of a person who softened her heart and chose to forgive. And her big, hurtful incident was merely an unexpected divorce. There are millions of other people throughout the world and throughout history who have courageously chosen to forgive and move on from experiences that were truly horrendous – things that were damaging to them physically, mentally and emotionally. Do a simple web search on the term "amazing stories of forgiveness" or something similar, or go to the web page www.theforgivenessproject.com/stories and you'll find examples of courage and forgiveness that will blow your heart open and move you to tears.

There are stories of people who have been victimized in extreme ways – shot, beaten, raped, imprisoned, kidnapped, tortured and otherwise violently abused. There are holocaust and genocide survivors, people who have seen loved ones brutally murdered, had their entire families and even communities mercilessly slaughtered. Yet these people have generated the ability to forgive the perpetrators of the crimes and atrocities in order to make peace within themselves. Not one of these once ordinary people *had* to forgive. Instead they *chose* to open their hearts and forgive and thus became truly extraordinary individuals as a result.

Freeing Yourself to Be Yourself

There is nothing, no event, no incident, no abandonment, hurt, crime or betrayal that's too big to forgive. When you decide to forgive a person or circumstance for you, then things will open up and something inside you will change. A light will shine into your mind and your heart, dispersing the darkness of hurt and judgment, revealing a pathway to forgiveness for yourself and all others involved. Through the power of your clear decision, intention and action, you'll find the means to set yourself free.

Again, it may be a process. You may need to approach the forgiveness as a project, and take it on in a step-by-step way over a period of days, weeks, months or even years to be fully complete and free of any lingering emotional residue and judgments. It depends on who or what you need to forgive, how much meaning, emotion and belief you've attached to it and how willing you are to surrender the role of the victim. Even the seeming biggest, most emotional, painful or traumatic events or experiences can be processed, digested and forgiven so that you're free of the lingering, limiting effects of them in your life.

Although forgiveness may take time and even feel hard, I promise you it's worth it. Let me remind you of some of the results and benefits of forgiving. Number one is freedom. The more you forgive yourself and others, the more free you'll feel and the more ability you'll have to express yourself in all ways in your life. Another is a greater possibility for connection with others and the ability to be authentic and intimate in your relationships. This leads also to more love and joy, happiness and feelings of fulfillment. Forgiveness opens the doors to more creativity and success as you break through and release the old emotional blockages that have encumbered your heart and mind. When you forgive, you regain access to the innate fullness of who you are and who you can be.

Forgiveness for the perpetrators of the big hurts, the greatest betrayals, the most traumatic events in your life is ultimately an act of self-love. And just like it did for Angela in the story above, the journey of forgiveness will lead you to destinations that you could never have imagined or experienced otherwise. True forgiveness endows you with freedom of the mind and heart, enabling life to surprise you, inspire you, and fill you with joy.

Freeing Yourself to Make a Difference

Forgiveness of the big hurts, the greatest betrayals and most traumatic events also offers the possibility of becoming an inspiring example, a beacon of hope and a powerful support to others. When you choose to look for and extract the lessons, wisdom or gifts offered by an experience – no matter how impossible that task might initially seem – you'll find ways of benefiting not only yourself but those around you too. Again, as with the story of Angela, her own painful divorce led her to train as a divorce coach. Her own crushing experience, once forgiven, gave her the ability to offer hope and support others to heal and move on from their broken relationships.

If you choose to make peace and move on, you'll find that your past traumas or painful experiences can become your biggest assets paying rich dividends not only to you, but to others as well. When forgiven and healed, they will endow you with an unparalleled level of compassion and understanding for people in similar situations. You'll find that the very incidents that once seemed to disable and diminish you, now empower you with the ability to make a positive difference in the lives of others. What you once may have viewed as solely a liability, will provide an invaluable contribution through you, sparking your ability to support, teach, guide or otherwise assist those going through similar experiences. When you choose to forgive for yourself, you ultimately benefit the greater whole.

If You Need It, Get Support

If you're in a situation where you're feeling a lot of struggle and pain, if the thought of trying to forgive someone or something feels unbearably big or difficult, it may be necessary to get some help. With the toughest hurts or issues, it can be useful to have a trusted person to support you along the path to forgiveness. That could be as simple as asking a compassionate, understanding friend or family member to listen and help you sort through your feelings. You might also benefit from some structured forgiveness work in a group process or with a coach trained specifically to be able to guide you step-by-step. For more information on forgiveness coaching options, go to www.forgivenessclub.com/forgiveness-coaching.

The most important thing is that you find someone who you can trust and feel safe with to help you work through the process. If the experience was very traumatic and your emotional wounds are deep, you may require the support of a skilled therapist or counselor to safely guide you through a healing process and bring you to a place where you can forgive. If you think that you may need that kind of support, at the end of this chapter I've included a few links to information and resources that might help you to identify an appropriate counselor or therapist for you.

If you choose to, you can take on and successfully complete any project of forgiveness. Regardless of how it occurs, forgiveness is an act of self-love. To forgive the people and situations of a major hurt or traumatic experience may take a lot of self-compassion, and it will certainly take resolve and a commitment to your choice to break free. Even though it may take some time to complete the process of forgiveness, once you decide and start on the path, you'll begin to experience relief and results. You'll begin to have more freedom, more energy, more hope and anticipation for living your life as you most want it to be.

Counseling / Therapy Resources

General Information

http://counsellingresource.com/

http://www.counselor.org/

Counselor/Therapist Search

http://therapists.psychologytoday.com/rms/prof_search.php

http://www.find-a-therapist.com/

Clifford B. Edwards

General Information and Counselor/Therapist Search

http://www.networktherapy.com/

http://psychcentral.com/

Forgiveness Journaling Exercise – Chapter 8

How can you apply the wisdom and gifts of your experience(s) to benefit yourself and others?

Once you've found the valuable lessons or wisdom gained through a past experience, there is a further step that can be taken. It's often not enough just to understand that there are lessons and wisdom to be gained from hurtful incidents of the past or present. To complete the cycle of learning, fully release your judgments and realize the true value of an experience, it's necessary to actually apply and use the knowledge in your life. The purpose of this exercise is to help you recognize how you can apply the lessons or wisdom gained in new or different ways for a greater benefit to yourself and others now and in the future.

On a new journal page, make a list of the value, benefits and lessons you can extract from one of the more painful or traumatic events from your past (refer back to your results from the exercise in Chapter 7 if need be). Then go back to each of the items on the list and begin to list or write about the various ways that you can apply it in your life in the present, and then into the future. As always, allow ideas and thoughts to come to you without editing them or trying to figure out what the answer is.

Present:

With a specific value/benefit list item in mind, look around the situations, activities and interactions of your life and ask yourself: "How can I use or apply this (information, insight, understanding, skill, quality, etc.) to help or benefit me in a way that hasn't occurred to me before?" Look particularly at the situations or circumstances that currently seem to be challenging to or difficult for you.

Once you have finished examining the situations and circumstances of your own life, you may continue by seeing how the same thing can be used or applied in meaningful ways for the benefit of family, friends, colleagues or others around you. Again ask, "How can I use or apply this (information, insight, understanding, skill, quality, etc.) to bring value and help me contribute to other people in my life?"

Future:

As above, go through each of the value/benefit items on your list and open up to thoughts and ideas for ways in which they might be able to serve you and/or contribute to others in the future. Allow yourself to connect with your deepest desires and dreams as you look ahead in your life. Notice if the lesson, wisdom or other value gained from this past experience has the potential to support you in ways that you might not have previously realized or imagined. You can ask yourself: "As I move forward in my life, how can I use this to benefit myself and others in new, useful, exciting or fulfilling ways?"

Continue writing until you've worked your way through the list. Then go back through your writing and identify one action step that you can take right now. What specifically can you do right now in your life to apply the value and benefit yourself and/or others? When you get at least one specific action that you're ready and willing to take, schedule it into your calendar and do it!

Chapter 9

What's the Relationship Between Apologizing and Forgiving?

Sincere forgiveness isn't colored with expectations that the other person apologize or change. Don't worry whether or not they finally understand you. Love them and release them. Life feeds back truth to people in its own way and time - just like it does for you and me.

-Sara Paddison

In this chapter we'll address the question: "What's the relationship between apologizing to someone and forgiving someone?" It might seem obvious, but let's go ahead and look into it a little more deeply anyway. When I apologize to someone, I'm saying, "I'm sorry about that." When I forgive, I'm saying, "That's over, I let that go, I'm not going to hold that against you."

Definitions

In order to help clarify and understand the two words, I again went to the Merriam-Webster online dictionary to get a formal definition for each. They are:

What's the Relationship between Apologizing and Forgiving?

<u>Apology</u>

1: a: a formal justification : DEFENSE

  b: EXCUSE

2: an admission of error or discourtesy accompanied by an expression of regret   <a public *apology*>

For the word "apology," it's the second definition that's most applicable in our context here. Although many times when people begin to apologize in the sense of definition two – offering an admission of error – they also quickly slip into apology in the first sense – justifying and defending their actions rather than offering an expression of regret. I don't know about you, but when that happens to me it doesn't feel like much of an apology. It feels more like they're only concerned with themselves and that they've just rubbed salt into the wound of the earlier offense. So in the context of forgiveness, I'm most interested in the form of apology that's offered sincerely in the spirit of taking responsibility for one's mistake or transgression and expressing regret or contrition for it.

<u>Forgive</u>

1: a: to give up resentment of or claim to requital for <*forgive* an insult>

  b : to grant relief from payment of <*forgive* a debt>

2: to cease to feel resentment against (an offender) : <u>PARDON</u><*forgive* one's enemies>

Just as in Chapter 1, the definitions 1:a and 2 stand out for the word "forgive," as they have to do with releasing or giving up resentment for some perceived insult or offense by another. Forgiveness is an act of letting go of the judgments and resentments towards another, and all the negative thoughts, feelings, beliefs and other baggage related to an experience or situation.

Forgiving

As stated in various ways throughout every chapter of this book, when you forgive, you clear the emotional, mental and spiritual burdens for yourself. Forgiveness is about letting go of the judgments, negative meanings, disempowering stories, hurt feelings, limitations and anything else that you might end up dragging around with you if you didn't forgive. It's about giving up the resentment, the blame, the anger, shame or guilt or anything else that might shut you down, dampen your life force and spirit, anything that would make you feel boxed in. The purpose of forgiving is to let go of anything that would rob you of your ability to be self-expressed and free, to have all the joy, connection and love that you want and deserve.

Apologizing

Apologizing and forgiving often go hand in hand and they're quite closely related. They can occur as the two sides of an interaction between an offender and the offended. Let's take a closer look at apologizing and then we'll see how they work together. When you apologize, you're offering an expression of responsibility, of sorrow, regret or contrition. You're saying,

"You know what, I screwed up, I'm sorry about that," or "I'm sorry I hurt you. I didn't mean to do that. "

It seems that I have opportunities to do that on a fairly frequent basis right at home, unfortunately. Not long ago, as I was talking with my wife, I made an offhand comment thinking that it would be funny. But when it tumbled out of my mouth I instantly knew it wasn't funny in that particular situation and context. My perception that it wasn't funny was validated by the look of hurt on my wife's face. As soon as I saw her expression, I knew I'd made a mistake. I also knew that there was the potential for a little hurt or even a small resentment to come between us and begin to affect our ability to communicate fully. So I apologized immediately. I said, "Honey, look, I'm sorry. I meant that comment to be funny and it obviously didn't come out that way. I didn't mean to hurt you, I apologize." And then I said, "Please forgive me."

Though an apology is addressed to another person or persons, I believe that as with forgiveness, when you apologize it's primarily for you. An apology allows you to clear out feelings of guilt, regret or shame that may otherwise linger and fester in your consciousness. It's also a way of clearing the air, clearing out negative or hurt feelings that might diminish your levels of communication, connection or intimacy with the other. You apologize so that you can reap the benefits of more open, authentic and effortless interactions. In that situation with my wife, my apology was for me to clear things up. I wanted to know that I had done what I could to make sure that there were no hard feelings, that there was nothing that might affect the closeness and natural flow our relationship.

Apologies and Amends

Sometimes more than just an apology is needed to clean things up between two parties. Sometimes after offering an apology, you may also find that you need to make amends of some sort. Making amends means setting things right between you both or making up for any loss that you might have caused the other through your actions. It is defined in Merriam-Webster online dictionary as:

<u>Amends:</u>

compensation for a loss or injury : RECOMPENSE

For an example, I'll go back to my college days again. One summer between school years, some friends and I got an apartment not far off campus. We built bunk bed frames, but needed mattresses to complete the beds. One night we climbed over the fence of one of the college's maintenance warehouses and made off with some mattresses we found stored outside the building. My friends picked from among the stack of well-used mattresses retrieved from dorm rooms. I, on the other hand, took a nice, brand new, plastic-wrapped one. At the time I managed to rationalize it as being okay. I made up some story to justify my theft of the mattress and assuage my feelings of guilt. I used the mattress for the entire summer before selling it to someone else when I moved out of the apartment.

Yet deep down I knew it was wrong to have stolen the mattress. Though I soon forgot about it and buried the memory, I unconsciously carried guilt and shame. Years later in a coaching exercise, this incident came up for me as something that weighed me down and made me feel unsettled. Though I was not specifically aware of it, the lingering regret caused me to feel bad about myself and lowered my self-esteem. I knew at the moment I recalled it that I needed to make amends. I went online and found a website for the manufacturer of the mattress that I'd pilfered over two decades previously. I looked up the current cost of a mattress of similar size and quality. Then I wrote a letter to the college comptroller to apologize and ask for forgiveness. To make amends, along with the letter I sent a check to cover the value of what I'd stolen, plus some interest. As soon as I did that, I immediately felt lighter and more free.

Through apologizing and making amends, I was able to release a burden of guilt and shame that I'd unconsciously carried for over twenty years. Just to conclude the story, a couple of weeks later I received a very nice response from the comptroller. He thanked me for the letter of apology for the theft, and told me that he respected my desire to make amends and clean it up. But for me it didn't matter whether I got any acknowledgement back from the school or not. I'd taken the action for my own peace of mind. I had simply done what I knew I needed to do in order to let it go and be free.

Requesting Forgiveness

A sincere apology often comes with a request for forgiveness, either spoken or unspoken. The request can be explicit if you specifically ask to be forgiven, as I did in my examples. Or the request can be implicit in the apology if it's not specifically verbalized. When you apologize to someone, it doesn't obligate them to forgive you. Neither should you deliver an apology with the expectation that you will be forgiven. Whether the other person chooses to respond in kind to the apology and opportunity to forgive is up to them. Apologizing for something you did is your choice. Forgiving you for the incident or offense is the choice of the other.

To be most effective, apologies need to be sincere in both meaning and intent and come as the result of your own choice. Both apologies and forgiveness are very personal things. As I've pointed out in previous chapters, forgiveness also may be a process that takes time. Even if you apologize, it may take a while for someone to get to the point of feeling ready and able to forgive you. And if they choose not to forgive, then the burden of negative feelings, meanings and beliefs is their responsibility to carry. If you apologize sincerely and, if necessary, make the amends that need to be made, then you no longer have any reason to carry a burden of guilt, shame or regret. You have done your part.

When someone offers an apology and asks to be forgiven – whether it's explicit or implicit – I'd recommend that you make the choice to do so. Even if someone never apologizes to you for an incident or experience that was hurtful in some way, you can still forgive. You can choose to forgive and let go of all of that emotion or feeling, because again forgiveness is for you. As I've stated so many times during this book, forgiveness is really not for the other person. Forgiveness is for you to let go of anything that might hold you back, limit you or prevent you from having the freedom and joy you want.

It's about Self-Forgiveness

Apologies can also be viewed as an integral part of self-forgiveness. You apologize to another person or party in part to relieve your own burden of guilt, regret, remorse or shame about your decisions or actions. In some situations, you may need to apologize to yourself, and then forgive yourself. Sometimes I have to do that. I have to say something like, "Oh Cliff, boy what was I thinking there? That was a mistake! I'm sorry." As I apologize to myself, choose not to judge and even make light of the situation, then I can forgive and let go. Self-forgiveness is a huge part of making sure that we're clean, clear and free to live joyfully and create bountifully. If you regularly choose both to apologize and forgive, you will avoid building up the residue of negative emotions and meanings from painful events both big and small.

I hope this offers a little more perspective and clarity on the topics of apologizing and forgiving. I also invite you to become more conscious of where you need to apologize to yourself and others, and then to *do* it. And see what happens as you do. To get some practice, do the apology exercise below. For more on forgiveness, go to www.forgivenessclub.com.

Forgiveness Journaling Exercise – Chapter 9

To whom and for what do you need to apologize and/or make amends?

The purpose of this exercise is to practice and experience the apology side of forgiveness. Just as there are people in your life you need to forgive, there are almost inevitably people you need to apologize to. It's very likely that from among the names on the list of people you need to forgive, there is someone to whom you need to offer an apology as well. This is especially true with the people in closest relationship to you – like parents, spouses/partners, children or other family members.

Softening your heart and apologizing to someone else for your own hurtful or inappropriate actions is a powerful first step toward being able to forgive yourself and the other fully and create a new kind of relationship with them for the future.

As you sit quietly with your journal or notebook, begin to make an Apology List. This is a list of people you've hurt or wronged in some significant way through your words, actions or inactions (you may refer to your list from the exercise in Chapter 1 to help identify candidates). When you think of a person or an event, if you feel guilt, shame, regret, embarrassment or other similar kinds of emotions, it's also an indication that you might need to apologize and ask for forgiveness.

Once you make the list, go back and for each person write down specifically what you need to apologize to them for. What exactly did you say or do that was hurtful or harmful to them? If you can't immediately think of something specific, then pause, gently breathe for a few moments and let your mind become quiet. Focus on your heart and ask yourself, "For what words, actions or inactions do I need to apologize to this person?" Then write down whatever comes to you, even if it doesn't make sense.

When you complete your Apology List, pick the name of one person as a place to begin. I suggest that you start with an apology that will be relatively easy to make, yet that still feels a bit challenging. Again sitting quietly, bring this person to mind and imagine their face. Focus your attention in the area of your chest, feeling your heart soften and bringing compassion toward yourself and this person. Ask yourself, "What do I need to say or share as an authentic apology?" Write it down making sure that you're simply taking responsibility for your hurtful actions toward the person and offering a humble apology.

If your actions caused some kind of tangible loss or cost to the other person, then determine if you need to make any kind of amends in order to complete the process of setting things right between the two of you. If you do, then come up with a straightforward and realistic plan for making recompense.

When you're finished considering and planning the apology (and amends if necessary), decide whether you'll deliver it in person, in a letter or some other way as appropriate. At this point, you may find it useful to share about your planned apology with a trusted person close to you, and ask for support or feedback. Once you've determined all the specifics and prepared in whatever way you need, pick a time and go do it!

Extra Credit:

To get the full value out of this exercise, go through the same process of planning and making an apology to all the other people on your Apology List. If your list is long, then you can make it a project to take on and do over time.

Chapter 10

I Can Forgive Someone Else, But How Can I Forgive Myself?

The truth is, unless you let go, unless you forgive yourself,
unless you forgive the situation, unless you realize that that
situation is over, you cannot move forward.
-Steve Maraboli

In this next-to-last chapter, I'm going to address a question that I think is of primary importance in the conversation of forgiveness. This is a question that you must understand and answer for yourself in order to gain the full range of benefits that are available through forgiveness. It's also something that I hear in various forms all the time. The question is: "I can forgive someone else, but how can I forgive myself?" Other versions of it are common too, like: "I'll never forgive myself for that." Or, "I don't know how I'm ever going to forgive myself for that."

All Forgiveness Is for You

I hate to hear people say things like that because of the self-limiting and self-punishing quality of the statements. Within this larger conversation of forgiveness, I cannot overstress the importance of self-forgiveness. As I've emphasized so often in earlier chapters, when you forgive someone else, it's really not about that other person. All forgiveness is really *about* you and *for* you. The point of forgiveness ultimately comes back to forgiving yourself. I have attempted to repeat this idea over and over in many ways so that even if you remember nothing else from this book in a few months, you will walk away with this concept. Forgiveness is about giving yourself the gift of freedom from the emotional burdens and attachments of the past. And until you forgive yourself, you're not free; you are still negatively attached and bound to incidents and events of your past. In order to be complete with forgiveness for any incident or circumstance, you must forgive yourself in addition to anyone else involved. The process of forgiveness starts and ends with self-forgiveness – with *you*.

Unfortunately, a lot of people don't understand this. You may still tend to think of forgiveness as something that you do solely for another person. You may think it's something that you're supposed to do to fix a relationship, to make peace or to help some other person feel better. Perhaps you've somehow been led to believe that you need to do this even at the expense of yourself and your own best interests. While improving a relationship or helping someone feel better can be a positive result of forgiveness, in the end when you forgive it's really all about your well-being. It's about enabling you to feel better and to increase your own sense of self-worth. It's about improving your relationship with yourself and being able to live more fully self-expressed, more responsibly and creatively.

Setting Yourself Free

Forgiveness – and specifically self-forgiveness – gives you the ability to move forward in your life more freely, unburdened of all of the weight of negative judgments, meaning and emotion from past experiences. It's about being able to let go of the shame, guilt, regret, anger, blame, resentment and whatever else you may be carrying around. Self-forgiveness is about releasing any remaining thought, judgment, belief or feeling that would weigh you down and hold you back. It's about giving yourself the levels of freedom, joy, light-heartedness and all of the other feelings and experiences you desire and deserve. When you forgive and free yourself of the past, you're able to choose and act more powerfully to create your life as you want it right here in the present and into the future.

I'll make a bold claim here. Forgiveness of yourself and others is the most important thing that you can do to have your life turn out the way you want it. When you forgive, you gain the freedom to live your life on your own terms. You release the righteous judgments, restricting beliefs and highly charged emotions that would limit you or keep you negatively connected to someone else. Self-forgiveness is the key to your self-constructed prison of past hurts and regrets. Forgiving yourself opens the doors to greater levels of success, self-expression and the fulfillment of your desires. It sets you free to have all of those things and so much more.

So how do you forgive yourself? Well, you forgive yourself in much the same way as you'd forgive someone else, because there really is no difference. As I discussed in Chapter 6, there are many different methods for forgiving. For small things, you may be able to forgive yourself with a simple choice to shift the meaning you've given to an incident, then let go of the negative judgments, thoughts and feelings and move on. For other, more significant things, you may need to approach the self-forgiveness as a process. But again, I want to emphasize that the secret to forgiving is to shift your perspective from that of the victim to that of a responsible, empowered human being. To begin to make that shift, you simply look for the life learning or wisdom you've gained or can gain through a negative experience. Any time that you can recognize and understand that a past hurtful experience has actually benefited you or will benefit you in some way, a shift will happen. It almost automatically clears the way for you to let go of the negative judgments, feelings and beliefs about the event and allows you to embrace the positive aspects. Life has presented me with many opportunities to do this. One of the most memorable had to do with the business I've referenced in earlier chapters.

My Big Failure

It was 1994 and the owner of the small, computerized litigation support services firm I worked for decided to close the business and return "in-house" as a corporate attorney. Rather than trying to find another job, I opted – with some trepidation – to start my own business in the same field. Fortunately, my former employer soon became my first client. She hired me to manage the documents for a litigation matter for her new employer, aerospace giant General Dynamics. Things went well and as time went along, other attorneys in her department and within another division of GD hired me too. Within about six months of starting the business, I had a full-time staff of three with additional project workers on call.

For about three years business was great. GD was going through both the sale of a division and a reorganization. The inevitable personnel lawsuits and related legal issues generated plenty of work for us. A few other corporations in the area and local law firms hired us as well. It was a busy, interesting time due to both the kinds of projects we were handling and the rapidly evolving technology tools available.

But by late 1997, our workload declined as most of the litigation related to reorganization and transition for GD wound down. The industry landscape had also changed as more law firms created technology groups competing with our services. I let go of all the project staff, and a couple of the full-time employees. With the workload continuing to fall, I reduced costs wherever I could. But despite the obvious warning signs, I took little action to market my services and gain new clients.

By the summer of 1998, the workflow had dwindled to a trickle and I remained as the sole employee of the business. I took on a few small joint venture projects with other companies, but the revenue wasn't enough. I dipped into my business line of credit to pay my own salary. Month by month I watched – seemingly helplessly – as the debt mounted and my once-profitable company spiraled closer to a crash. But rather than feeling motivated to work hard, find new customers and generate revenue, I distracted myself with trivial tasks and surfing the web. I cut my own wages in half to slow the accumulation of debt. Soon thereafter as I cut my salary again, I began to experience anxiety attacks. With each day I felt more resigned and depressed. I blamed myself for the failure and judged myself as incompetent, lazy, stupid and worse.

In desperation, I hired an executive coach to help me face my challenges and turn things around. Though it seemed strange at the time, the first thing he did was guide me through an exercise to identify my core personal values. Next, he had me create a vision for my life as I ideally wanted it to be. From these two exercises it became clear that the litigation support services field no longer held any enjoyment or passion for me. In fact, I realized that I really disliked the legal field. With that understanding, I began to see why I had barely tried to do effective marketing and bring in new clients.

I also realized that the process of coaching was something I had a natural affinity and talent for. It was something I'd been doing with others most of my life without knowing it. Invigorated with a new sense of purpose and encouraged by my own coach, I decided to forge a new career. I took coach training classes, joined the two local professional coaching organizations and began to develop a practice of my own. As my coaching activities grew, my old business withered and died. Only five and a half years after starting the company, I sold the remaining equipment and transitioned one last project to a joint venture partner.

A New Beginning

Though free from the business, I was left with many thousands of dollars in company debt. Despite the passion and excitement for my new career, I continued to make myself wrong for having failed at the old. With each bank statement I blamed and berated myself for not having worked harder or done something differently. Every time I allowed my mind to wander into the past, I became angry, depressed and regretful about how I'd squandered the opportunity of the old business. Ironically, while encouraging others to have great lives and develop self-loving, self-supportive practices, I routinely buried my own negative feelings and judgments under mountains of activity and distraction and self-medicated with glasses of wine. Despite my desire and efforts to let go of the shame and regret, true self-forgiveness eluded me.

I became successful in the field of coaching and training, growing both personally and professionally. But throughout the first few years, I still carried the heavy burden of self-blame, regret and recrimination about my failed business. Then while participating in a group exercise during a seminar one day, something happened. I had a shift in perspective about my "failure" that allowed me to see it in a new way. The breakthrough came when I acknowledged how happy I was as a coach and trainer. I loved the work, the people around me and my life! I realized that had my old business continued to operate and generate income, I wouldn't have hired a coach. I wouldn't have started training and practicing as a coach and I wouldn't be there feeling happy and content in that moment! I would likely still be trudging along in an unwanted, unsatisfying career. I understood at a deep level that I *had to* fail in my old business - one I really disliked - in order to find success and fulfillment doing something I loved.

In that moment of insight everything transformed. I could see that my perceived "failure" was simply a step in my life - one that actually came with a great gift and blessing. Failing had given me the freedom to pursue work that felt good and made me happy. With that realization and the profound shift in perspective, I forgave myself for allowing my business to fail. I was able to immediately let go all of the negative judgments about myself in relation to that old business. I ceased blaming myself, and ceased resenting and regretting my actions and decisions. I experienced an instantaneous release of the emotional load I'd carried for years. I gave up the burden of negative emotions, thoughts and beliefs, and instead saw the entire experience in the light of gratitude and appreciation.

In finally understanding the gift and benefit of the experience in the overall landscape of my life, everything had shifted. This was true self-forgiveness, not just some flimsy rationalization to temporarily dilute the negative feelings. I was finally able to feel complete and at peace about my long-defunct business. I now remember the experience as something positive, beneficial and serving to me.

In order to be truly forgiven, complete and at peace with an experience, you must forgive yourself. There's no freedom until you've released your own burdens of the heart and mind. If you're still holding judgments, anger, guilt, shame or negative beliefs about yourself, then you're not complete with a situation. You haven't left the experience in the past, which means you're still carrying it with you in the present. Any time that you're carrying around this kind of baggage from the past, you are burdened with an unnecessary load. You're weighing yourself down, expending your precious energy, and limiting your ability to create, achieve and enjoy what you desire.

Recognize the Burden

In a moment, I'm going to ask you to close your eyes, relax your body and do a little exercise of the imagination to get an idea of the weight of the burdens you need to release through self-forgiveness. Please read through the steps of this short exercise below, then close your eyes and complete it.

1. Remember some of the biggest personal mistakes you've made in your life that you've not yet forgiven. What are the decisions in your past that cost you or hurt you in some way, things that you regret or feel shameful about? Recall the choices you've made that you still feel angry or frustrated with yourself about, or that are still otherwise emotionally significant and lingering with you.

2. Recall any of the negative or hurtful things you've done to others throughout your life that you haven't forgiven yourself for. What are the incidents in which you injured or caused hurt to someone else, the things that you feel guilty about, blame yourself for or are still affecting you in a negative or limiting way.

3. Imagine that all of that is piled on top of you, that you're actually loaded down and carrying it all with you wherever you go.

4. Allow yourself to feel the emotional and even the physical weight of it. Feel the burden that these old, unresolved and unforgiven experiences place on you.

5. Feel what it does to your body to have to still hold onto and carry all of that old stuff with you right here in the present. Feel what it does to your sense of power, confidence and well-being. Breathe and feel it.

6. Take a deep breath, then open your eyes and continue reading.

The first time I did this exercise, my shoulders immediately started to feel tight and tired and my body felt like it was drained of energy. It seemed hard to even generate the will to move, let alone to go out, achieve my goals and live the life of my dreams. What happened for you as you did this just now?

If there are things from your past that you haven't forgiven yourself for, you're burdened unnecessarily and reducing your overall effectiveness in life. You're still carrying the weight and encumbrance of all of that no longer relevant stuff with you. Just imagine how much of your energy goes into carrying, managing and dealing with all of that.

Quantify It

In fact, you can even do another little exercise - a little meter reading - that will show you how much of your life force you are using to hold onto and maintain those burdens of the past.

1. Take a moment to close your eyes again and imagine a little gauge right in front of you that reads from 0 to 100. Let this gauge represent the totality of your innate life energy.

2. Now allow it to show you as a percentage, exactly how much of your energy you expend on the pointless activity of dragging around your unforgiven experiences of the past.

3. Read your energy meter - again as a percentage of your total life force energy - and remember that number.

4. Take another breath, open your eyes and continue reading.

What does your gauge tell you? The first time I did this exercise my little meter read at about 75%. That meant that it took about three quarters of my total available life force energy just to drag around and manage the weight of the hurts, feelings and other unforgiven "stuff" from my past. All of a sudden it made sense to me that I often felt exhausted, frustrated and as if every activity I engaged in was a struggle. I could see that I was trying to live a full and productive life with only about 25% of my energy actually available to do so and that I was uselessly expending the rest. I made a commitment right then and there to start to reclaim and use my valuable, essential life force only for projects and activities that are worthwhile and enjoyable.

For other people I've done this meter exercise with, the reading has been as low as 30 - 40% and as high as 90 - 95% of their available life force energy wasted on dragging around the burdens of the past! If you feel tired all the time, or feel stuck and unable to generate the kind of life you want, do you think this might help explain why? Think about what it costs you to hold on to the grudges, resentments, blames, shame, guilt and other negative judgments and beliefs of the past. Consider what you've given up to carry that burden with you each and every day of your life. Think about other things you don't have the energy or will to pursue because of that burden: perhaps your dreams, happiness or more intimate, fulfilling relationships. That's no way to live. So if you're struggling in your life, if you feel like you lack the drive, motivation and energy to make the changes you want and to create the life that you want, then self-forgiveness likely holds the key for you.

Choose to Let it Go

Now we're going to finish this exercise of the imagination, so once again read the steps below and then close your eyes for a moment while you go through them.

1. Now imagine letting all those burdens drop away and return to the past where they belong. Imagine them dissolving, falling off of you and fading into the recesses of the past.

2. See how you feel when you picture yourself with all of that unforgiven, unresolved stuff gone. How much lighter do you feel? How much more energy do you have?

3. Look at your little energy meter now to see what it reads. How much of your life force is available to you? How much more might you be able to accomplish? How much more alert and nimble could you feel, both mentally and physically?

4. Now imagine going through every day like this.

    a. Imagine getting up in the morning feeling energized and excited to start the day.

    b. You move through the activities of your day with a spring in your step, feeling light-hearted, confident and free to do what you want and need to do.

c. You have a self-assured smile on your face and a huge confident grin inside. You express yourself naturally and easily, and you know intuitively what's right for you and what you need to avoid.

d. People look at you and recognize that there's something different about you. You have a special something that they don't have – something that they can't quite identify, but they know it's something that *they want* too.

This is what self-forgiveness can give you. Self-forgiveness can and will give you those levels of freedom, lightness, confidence, energy and power.

In the practice of self-forgiveness, you must start with a decision. It's a decision to cultivate self-love and self-worth. Self-forgiveness is a natural outcome of choosing to feel good about yourself and choosing to love yourself completely. When you love yourself, it's only natural that you would want to let go of the burdens of the past. It's natural that you would want to fully express yourself and bring all that you have to offer to every moment, to every interaction, to every relationship and to every project you undertake. Imagine how great that would feel!

Now you know you can forgive someone else, and you have great reasons to forgive yourself. So please, begin to give yourself the gift of self-forgiveness today. To support you in that endeavor, I've included a special exercise for you below. For additional inspiration to forgive and stories of the success of others, go to: www.forgivenessclub.com/stories.

Forgiveness Journaling Exercise – Chapter 10

Giving the gift of self-forgiveness.

This exercise is designed to support you to forgive yourself for a situation from your past where there are still negative judgments, feelings and beliefs you're dragging around with you. In this exercise you'll be writing a forgiveness letter to yourself. The purpose of the letter is to express on paper anything and everything that you need to in order to be able to process through the experience, shift your perspective, and recognize the value and benefit of it so you can forgive yourself completely. (Allow yourself 30 – 45 minutes to finish this exercise.)

Sit down in a quiet place with your notebook or journal. As you breathe easily, bring to mind a situation in which you feel like you really screwed up or did something terribly wrong. This would be an event that you regret, feel guilty or shameful about, and for which you have lingering, nagging blame or anger toward yourself. When you get the specific event or experience, write it down at the top of your page with the prefix: "I choose to forgive myself for..."

Write a forgiveness letter to yourself.

As you prepare to write the forgiveness letter, begin by breathing slowly and consciously for a few moments. As you do, imagine your heart opening and softening toward yourself. Imagine mentally and emotionally stepping up and out of the usual patterns of negative thought and judgment that you hold about this event or circumstance. Once you feel a bit more compassionate and clear, it's time to begin the letter.

Write this letter as a journaling exercise, free-writing rather than thinking it through or planning it carefully. What you'll find below is a suggested outline. You can modify or add to this anything that you need in order to feel forgiven, free and at peace.

Opening:

Dear _____ (fill in your own name),

I now choose to forgive myself for _____ (fill in the blank).

Body:

Continue the letter by describing the circumstances of the event - what happened and what did you do that you blame yourself for? Then describe the old meaning and judgments you'd made about the event, and share the way that it made you think and feel about yourself. In a new paragraph, describe how those negative thoughts, judgments and feelings limited you or extracted a cost in your life.

For the next section, imagine and then describe how you will feel and what else you'll be able to do as you forgive yourself, free yourself, reclaim your energy and give up the burdens of the past. Write this in present tense, as if you're in that forgiven and free state right now, feeling, seeing and experiencing everything you're describing.

Next, begin to write about the lessons, wisdom and other ways in which the experience has benefited you. Spend a lot of time in this section and write down anything that comes to you regardless of whether or not it seems to make sense. Now look ahead to the future and write about the ways in which you can apply these lessons and benefits to move forward in your life and to make a contribution to others in some way.

Apologies:

Write an apology for all of the burdens you placed on yourself. Apologize for the negative judgments and thoughts or for any hurtful, self-sabotaging words and behaviors toward yourself. If there's someone else you need to apologize to or if there are amends you need to make, acknowledge it here too.

Closing:

Write a loving, compassionate and understanding statement of forgiveness to yourself. Say thank you for giving yourself the gift of this forgiveness letter. Make a promise to use the lessons, wisdom and new perspectives gained. Express anything else you need to in order to feel complete and at peace. Close with an open-hearted, compassionate and caring declaration of self-love. Then sign your name.

When you're finished with the letter, sit with it for a few minutes and bask in the new feelings of freedom and possibility that come with self-forgiveness. Now you may either keep the letter as a cherished memento, or ceremoniously burn it as a symbol of your release and completion of this past event.

Chapter 11

Conclusion

People are often unreasonable and self-centered.
Forgive them anyway.
-Mother Teresa

In the previous chapters, I've focused mainly on the individual aspects of forgiveness, pointing out what forgiveness is, why you should forgive and how you can do it. I've also attempted to be as clear and emphatic as possible in explaining the benefits available to you through forgiving yourself and others. But the individual choice to forgive and the individual results of forgiveness are just a part of the larger picture. It's merely a step towards what I see as the most pressing need.

An Unforgiving World

Forgiveness is something that is desperately needed in our world today. Look around you, read or watch the news, indulge in popular media and you'll see lots of conflict, hatred, anger, resentment and blame. You'll also see behaviors revealing long-lasting patterns of guilt, shame, regret and resignation. All of these affect people at a group level as well as individually.

Conclusion

Everywhere we see entities like political parties, religious groups, governments and other kinds of organizations locked in conflict with or in struggle against one another. Almost inevitably, the conflict and struggle is rooted in some offense or grievance of the past. Further, it's often based on some individual or collective grudge or resentment that is no longer relevant, but that has simply been carried forward from times past to color and inform the interactions of the present.

Then if you zoom in from the group to the individual level and look at the citizens of the world - both your neighbors and those spread throughout every country on the globe - you'll notice billions of people who are burdened, encumbered and limited by the weight of guilt, shame regret and remorse they carry. There are countless people who suffer with hearts smoldering in anger, resentment and blame, nurturing grudges and righteous indignation.

As a result, we live in a world filled with so many problems that seem difficult and intractable. We live with issues on so many levels that are stressful, painful, tremendously costly and even deadly. We live in a world in which war, hatred and violence are considered to be inevitable. But what if they really are unnecessary? What if there were a path to freedom, understanding and cooperation available instead?

The cost of non-forgiveness is great and I believe that it's a cost we can no longer continue to bear given the kinds of challenges and issues we face as individuals, organizations, societies and as a species. The entrenched cultural, political and religious ways of thinking, acting and interacting are leading us collectively down a path to disaster. We're at a turning point in the world and in the history of mankind environmentally, economically and socially. We have to learn to come together, give up the grudges and resentments of the past, and focus on our commonalities rather than our differences in order to make our way forward into a manageable and survivable future.

The Solution Starts with You

The solution to freedom from so many of the problems, struggles and conflicts is forgiveness. This solution is simple, readily available and something that you're now very familiar with. Individually and collectively, forgiveness is the key to liberation of the mind and heart. Forgiveness offers the means of freeing ourselves and our world from the patterns and burdens of the past and opening the doors to the possibility of a brighter, more peaceful and fulfilling future. Debbie Ford, an author, transformational leader and personal friend and mentor, once wrote: "Forgiveness is the hallway between the past and the future." If humans and other species are to survive and thrive on our one and only planet over the next fifty, 100 or 200 years and beyond, then we must choose to boldly diverge from the ways of the past to create a new, cooperative and sustainable future.

We each have to choose to let go of our own righteous judgments, rigid perspectives and the obsessive desire to win or be right at the expense of others. We must reject the old collective mindset of victim and victimizer. We have to choose to open our minds and hearts to the ideas, possibilities and realities that are only available through reconciliation and cooperation. We now, more than ever, need to individually and collectively commit to encouraging and practicing forgiveness - today, tomorrow and every day. We each must become models of how to be open hearted, compassionate and forgiving, thus becoming examples of the change we want to see in the world at large.

Further, we need to engage those around us in conversations of forgiveness. We must teach and support our children, family members, friends and colleagues to open their minds and hearts to the concepts and practices of forgiveness so that they too may reap the benefits of greater freedom, peace of mind, confidence, happiness, creativity and success. We have to break out of any past conditioning of resentment, anger, righteous judgments and desire for revenge, to become champions of a more compassionate, understanding, resourceful and connected way of being on the planet.

This is the vision I hold and am working to advance through the Forgiveness Club. Founded in July of 2012, the Club's purpose statement is:

Promoting, Exploring, Teaching and Supporting
Concepts and Practices of Forgiveness for Our World

The Forgiveness Club is a place where people committed to compassionate, forgiving and future-oriented ways of thinking, acting and interacting can come for support, encouragement, tools and information. Within the Forgiveness Club site, you'll find articles, videos, audios, links to resources and other useful materials. It's also intended to be a community, a place to gather, to interact, to exchange ideas, to seek help with challenges, share stories and celebrate successes. My desire is that the Forgiveness Club be part of a larger movement of people, interests and organizations all dedicated to breaking free from the past. Members of the Forgiveness Club are committed individually and collectively to bring more peace, understanding, cooperation and responsible action to our world through the practice of forgiveness and clear, direct communication.

If you've gotten value from the information, ideas and tools in this Forgiveness Handbook, please go join and explore the Forgiveness Club now at: www.forgivenessclub.com. By doing so, I'll also be able to keep you informed of upcoming events, activities, new products and services designed to support you in accessing more choices and opportunities in your life through the development of a "forgiven and free" mindset.

I take the bold and hopeful position that anything – any hurt, any betrayal any offense – can and should be forgiven. Forgiving yourself and others opens the doors to new possibilities and new realities. Freedom of thought, choice and action is your birthright. You deserve to leave the bondage of the past behind and open yourself up to greater and more joyful expressions of who and what you are. You also have a responsibility to do your part to set our world on a more peaceful and harmonious path for future generations.

Forgiveness is the key to all of that and more, and you never have to do it alone. Specifically to provide structured support to help you forgive, I've developed and teach what I call the *Ladder of Freedom* Forgiveness Coaching Process. It is a step-by-step process that you can go through to assist you in coming to grips with, shifting perspective on and forgiving any significantly hurtful situations or incidents. It can help you make peace with events of the past and find the gifts of the experiences that occurred as deeply painful and traumatically life-altering. I'll feature the *Ladder of Freedom* in an upcoming book, but if you want more information about it now, go to www.forgivenessclub.com/forgiveness-coaching. There you'll find other resources for accessing the level of support you need to process through, heal and ultimately forgive anything from your past or present.

Now that you've come to the end of this book, it's time for you to take action. It's time for you to commit to a new way of thinking, choosing and acting in this regard. You can decide to take on forgiveness for your own benefit, for the benefit of those close to you or for the benefit of the world. You can actually achieve all three at once! In fact, when you forgive, you automatically do. Because no matter what motivates you to adopt the perspectives and practices of forgiveness, everyone benefits and everyone wins. Don't put it off: make a new commitment and take some empowering, forgiving action today.

A Note from the Author

I'm writing this extra note literally days before publishing this book in both print and electronic formats. Last week I began a course of chemotherapy to treat an indolent, follicular B-cell lymphoma that has taken hold in my body. I was diagnosed with it almost 2 years ago and was then put into a period of what my oncologist refers to as "watchful waiting," as we monitored the cancer to see if it would progress to the point where medical treatment became necessary.

Shortly after being diagnosed, I drew a connection between my development of cancer and a number of unforgiven and un-resolved incidents in my life that I had either denied or failed to recognize. It made perfect sense. Despite that I knew a lot about forgiveness and had even done a lot of forgiving, there were still people and incidents from my past that I hadn't fully forgiven. So I continued to carry negative judgments and beliefs, buried resentments, repressed anger, guilt and shame – all of which contributed to emotional stress and toxicity in my body. It was an unconscious burden of stress and toxicity. Yet over time it diminished the healthy functioning of my immune system and affected my well-being in other ways.

Not coincidentally, lymphoma is a cancer of the immune system, so I can easily find a relationship between it and the negative judgments, hidden grudges and resentments, denied guilt and shame. I'm not naming these things as *the cause*, but as contributing factors. I believe the effects of unconscious stress from repressed feelings and emotional toxicity from the negative thoughts and beliefs of non-forgiveness can contribute to the development of cancers and other diseases. We are just not meant to exist day to day with the unconscious mental, emotional and spiritual burdens imposed by non-forgiveness.

Shortly after my diagnosis, I began to focus more energy and attention on forgiving and forgiveness. That focus led me to write The Forgiveness Handbook. Exploring the concepts and writing it has been part of my therapeutic journey. I made other changes in diet, attitude and lifestyle also aimed at reducing the amount of conscious and unconscious stress and toxicity. Still the time has come for medical treatment. So now I'll be receiving the chemotherapy treatments for about 7 months, followed by maintenance doses for another 8 months. I'm happy to say that the prognosis is good and I fully expect the cancer to go into remission for many years or even decades as a result. But I have to wonder, what would have happened if I had fully forgiven myself and others much earlier in my life? With a body and immune system uncompromised by that form of stress and toxicity, would I be in this situation now?

I hadn't originally planned to share about the cancer here in The Forgiveness Handbook. The question and answer format, the concepts and examples, the cajoling and encouraging seemed like enough to prompt more of you onto the path of forgiveness. Besides, I'm planning another book to write about this lymphoma journey, so why bring it up at all? But as I started the chemo I knew that I had to share at least a glimpse of this experience here and now. So I offer this note partially as caution and partially as inspiration. Don't wait to forgive. Don't assume that you've forgiven all that you need to forgive. Use the ideas, information and exercises of this book to lighten your load, free your heart and mind and indeed to eliminate a huge source of unconscious stress and emotional toxicity. You don't need to experience disease (dis-ease) to seek the release of forgiveness. Choose the path of forgiveness for the many other benefits and gifts that it brings. For that certainly is enough.

Clifford Edwards, June 26, 2013

Acknowledgments

I want to start by thanking my wife Loree, for her enduring love, support, and feedback as I was writing the book and especially for her patience during our years together as I've learned about forgiveness through many experiences of trial and error with her and others.

I need to acknowledge Debbie Ford, as a mentor, teacher and the inspiration for me to share my own experiences and perspectives on this topic, as well as for the tremendous body of knowledge and experience I gained through 12 years of working with her at The Ford Institute for Integrative Coaching. In addition I want to thank my former staff colleagues at the Institute, Jeff Malone, Donna Lipman, Julie Stroud and Kelley Kosow for their insights, support and contributions over the years.

Thanks to my book editor John Harten, who offered great feedback, raised the bar and challenged me to produce something much more clear and useful than what I'd initially produced. Gratitude goes also to Elise Reid who worked through multiple cover design iterations to come up with the brilliantly appropriate and elegantly simple olive branch theme. I'm grateful as well to Angela for fearlessly sharing her own story as teaching example. Thanks to online resources, brainyquote.com, goodreads.com and merriam-webster.com for many of the quotes and definitions used herein.

Thank you to my friends/colleagues Adam Heller and Rev. Jerry Troyer for their encouragement and generosity in sharing lessons learned through their own book publishing experiences. Thanks also to Mike Koenigs and the entire crew at Instant Customer for ideas, training and support related to publishing and marketing this book.

Finally, I need to express appreciation and give so much credit to my former students, training program participants and all my individual coaching clients throughout the years. Thank you for the bountiful gifts of insight and understanding you delivered to me due to your courage, willingness, diligence and sharing as we worked together through so many processes of personal growth and forgiveness. You are truly the ones this book was written by and for.

The Olive Branch

Since the days of ancient Greek civilization, the olive branch has been a symbol of peace. This symbolism of the olive branch has remained consistent to the present day and is used and recognized as such in cultures and societies throughout the world. When proffered from one person to another, it is considered to be an offer and request to settle differences, make peace and seek reconciliation.

I believe that forgiveness is the path necessary to achieve lasting peace and meaningful reconciliation. Therefore I chose to use the olive branch as a fitting and evocative thematic image for this book on forgiveness.

About the Author

Clifford Edwards has been a professional coach, mentor, trainer and consultant in continuous practice for over fifteen years. Along with best-selling author and thought leader Debbie Ford, Cliff co-founded the Ford Institute for Integrative Coaching in 2000. Serving as a staff member, trainer and key architect of the Institute's programs for twelve years, he helped develop numerous innovative, effective coaching models and methodologies, and train over 1000 life coaches worldwide.

As an author, Cliff draws on his own life experiences, extensive knowledge and rich personal development background to write with compassion and clarity. He produces books, processes and programs to help people become more self-aware, accepting, loving and confident so that they can have greater success, more freedom, improved communications, better relationships, and a more profound sense of joy and fulfillment in their lives.

For his clients and students, Cliff offers life-changing perspectives, supports clear, definitive actions and provides breakthrough results. He is committed to the life-long process of self-discovery and strives to be an example of what's possible through continuing to stretch outside of the comfortable confines of past thoughts and beliefs.

Cliff lives in San Diego, California, where he shares a home with his wife Loree and warrior princess cat, Athena.

<u>Also by Clifford B. Edwards</u>

The Forgiveness Handbook Companion Workbook - Simple Exercises for Freedom of the Mind and Heart
<u>www.theforgivenesshandbook.com/workbook</u>

Made in the USA
San Bernardino, CA
15 October 2013